*TWAYNE'S WORLD AUTHORS SERIES*

*A Survey of the World's Literature*

Sylvia E. Bowman, Indiana University

GENERAL EDITOR

# CHINA

William Schultz, University of Arizona

EDITOR

# Lu You

*TWAS 427*

# LU YOU

### By MICHAEL S. DUKE
*University of Vermont*

**TWAYNE PUBLISHERS**
A DIVISION OF G. K. HALL & CO., BOSTON

**Library of Congress Cataloging in Publication Data**

Duke, Michael S
    Lu You.

    (Twayne's world authors series; TWAS 427: China)
    Bibliography: pp. 153–56
    Includes index.
    1. Lu, Yu, 1125–1210—Criticism and interpretation.
PL2687.L8Z74      895.1'1'4      76–43052
ISBN 0–8057–6267–1

MANUFACTURED IN THE UNITED STATES OF AMERICA

*Dedicated*
*with all my love*
*to*
Ch'i Li-chuang Duke
*zhi qi xiong,*
*shou qi ci.*

# Contents

# About the Author

Michael S. Duke received the Ph.D. degree from the Department of Oriental Languages at the University of California, Berkeley. From 1974–76, he has taught Chinese literature, language, and survey courses in aspects of Chinese culture at the George Washington University in Washington, D. C. He is currently on the faculty at the University of Vermont.

Professor Duke's reviews and articles have appeared in *Literature East and West.*

# Preface

This book is intended to introduce the English-speaking audience to the *shi* or lyric poetry of Lu You (1125–1210), the acknowledged master of the genre during the Southern Sung dynasty (1126–1279). It is also hoped that this study will correct the commonly held misconception of Lu You as merely or even primarily a "patriotic poet" (*ai-guo shi-ren*). As a result of three years of reading and study of his entire canon of some 10,000 *shi* poems I have attempted to give a balanced and fair representation of the scope and relative importance *for Lu himself* of his various poetic themes. Except for one very famous *ci* or "Lyric Meter" poem, "Phoenix Hairpin" (*chai-tou-feng*), all of the poems translated here are in the *shi* style.

Without giving a detailed explanation of classical Chinese prosody, let me briefly explain the basic *shi* forms. Aside from four character per line verse, which Lu never wrote, the earliest traditional form he employed was the Ancient Verse (*gu-shi*) form which has either five or seven characters per line, contains an indefinite number of lines, usually rimes on the even-numbered lines, and employs either one rime throughout or varies the rime as desired for particular effects. Lu most frequently wrote Ancient Verse poems having eight, twelve, sixteen, or twenty lines with a rime change every four lines corresponding to a change in thought or subject and giving a nearly stanzaic effect. The *yue-fu* or Music Bureau style may be considered a subclass of Ancient Verse and its use is explained in Chapter 3. The other major form Lu employed was Regulated Verse (*lü-shi*), also known as the Modern Style (*jin-ti*), which was especially perfected by Du Fu and the poets of the Tang dynasty (618–907). Regulated Verse poems have five or seven characters per line, are limited to eight lines only, employ the same rime throughout, usually rime on the even-numbered lines with minor variations permitted, require that the four middle lines must form two grammatically parallel and tonally antithetical couplets, and have a fixed tone pattern, again allowing for some minor variations. Quatrains (*jue-ju*) are basically the same as Regulated Verse except for the number of lines. It is characteristic of Lu's mature style that he employed both parallelism and antithesis (called *dui-zhang* or *dui-ou* in Chinese) even in his Ancient Verse poems where such practice was not strictly required. For a detailed discussion of classical Chinese prosody James J. Y. Liu's *The Art of Chinese Poetry* (University of Chicago Press, 1962) is still the best introduction.

I have devoted Chapter 1 to a brief biography and a discussion of the major characteristics of Lu's personal and social concerns—his patriotic sentiments; the legend of his romantic eccentricities; and his interest in Daoist religion, alchemy, and occult phenomena. Chapter 2, the longest in the book, traces the origins and development of Lu's poetic style and his image of himself as a poet from his early imitation of the Jiangxi School poets through the fervent realism of his patriotic verse to the transcendent imagery of his pastoral and Daoist inspired poetry. Chapters 3 through 7 then present translations and critical comments and analyses of representative groups of poems arranged according to Lu's most commonly used themes: patriotism, Daoism and alchemy, drinking wine, response to nature, and dreams. The true importance of patriotic verse in his entire canon can be clearly seen from these chapters. The personal and Daoistic themes of the final four chapters, especially that on dream poetry, bulk larger than patriotism for his mature style and present a side of his personality and poetry too often overlooked or even deliberately distorted in recent Chinese works. I hope that I have demonstrated that both Lu's personality and his creative work were far more sophisticated and complex than the traditionally applied epithet "patriotic poet" would indicate.

I would like to thank Professors Cyril Birch, James Miller, and Wolfram Eberhard of the University of California, Berkeley, and Professor William Schultz of the University of Arizona for all of their help in the preparation of this work. Professor Miller's guidance and comments on the translation of Chinese poetry have been of immeasurable assistance to me. I only hope that my translations live up to his expectations as well as *dui-de-qi*

## Preface

Lu You's great poetic genius. My debt to Professor Birch goes back many years and covers much more than just this work or even strictly academic matters. His example and his concern have been of great inspiration and encouragement to me and I thank him very much for them. Professor Eberhard's erudite comments on various aspects of Sung society have helped me to correct several erroneous impressions concerning Lu's life and times that were present in my original doctoral dissertation. Professor Schultz, my editor, has helped very much in the organization of this my first book. Of course none of these men are responsible for whatever errors must inevitably remain in the text, and I trust that my colleagues in the field will graciously point them out to me.

# Acknowledgments

For permission to quote extensively from copyrighted works, I wish to express my gratitude to the following:

Columbia University Press for portions reprinted from *The Complete Works of Chuang Tzu,* translated by Burton Watson. Copyright © 1968 Columbia University Press.

Harper and Row, Publishers, Inc. for material from *The Forge and the Crucible: The Origins and Structures of Alchemy,* by Mircea Eliade and translated from the French by Stephen Corrin. Copyright © 1962 by Rider and Company and published as a Harper Torchbook edition in 1971.

Harvard University Press for material from *An Introduction to Sung Poetry* by Kojiro Yoshikawa and translated from the Japanese by Burton Watson. Copyright © 1967 by the Harvard-Yenching Institute.

Pantheon Books for material from two books: *Memories, Dreams, Reflections* by Carl Gustav Jung, recorded and edited by Aniela Jaffe and translated from the German by Richard and Clara Winston. Copyright © 1961, 1962, 1963 by Random House, Inc. Published as Vintage Number V-268.

*Psychotherapy East and West* by Alan W. Watts. Copyright © 1961 by Pantheon Books, a Division of Random House, Inc. Published as a Ballantine Book, 01642.095.

# Chronology

1125    November 13 (seventeenth day of tenth lunar month)
        Lu You born in a boat on the banks of the Huai River.
1126    Fall of the Northern Sung dynasty to the Jürched-Jin.
1127    Emperor Gao-zong began the Southern Sung dynasty.
1144–   Lu married childhood sweetheart Tang Wan, but mother
1145    forced a divorce. Later he married Miss Wang.
1148    Lu studied poetry with Zeng Ji for seven years.
1153    Placed first in provincial examinations, but dropped
        from the list due to the anger of Qin Kui.
1155    "Phoenix Hairpin" (*chai-tou-feng*) incident.
1161    First Sung-Jin war in his lifetime: Jin aggression repulsed
        by Sung forces under Liu Qi and Yu Yun-wen.
1162    Lu given first audience with new Emperor Xiao-zong and
        awarded honorary *jin-shi* degree.
1163–   Second Sung-Jin war: Sung counterattack ends in defeat.
1164
1170    Sent to Kui-zhou in Sichuan. Wrote the *Ru-shu-ji*.
1172    Spent eight months in Nan-zheng as advisor to Chief
        Pacification Officer Wang Yan. Transferred to be advisor
        in Chengdu. Visited Daoist recluse Shang-guan Dao-ren
        on Green Wall Mountain in Sichuan.
1175    Bought a house by the Flower Washing Stream in Cheng-
        du near site of Du Fu's Thatched Hut. Two year friend-
        ship with Fan Cheng-da began. Lu styled himself "Reck-
        less Old Man" (*Fang-weng*).
1189    Guang-zong took the throne. Lu called to edit the *Veri-
        table Records of Gao-zong*. Impeached for third time and
        began final retirement.
1194    Xiao-zong died, Guang-zong refused to mourn and was
        forced from office by Zhao Ru-yu and Han Tuo-zhou
        who placed Ning-zong on the throne. Intensified faction-
        alism.

1202 Lu called to Hangzhou to edit *Veritable Records* of Xiao-
zong and Guang-zong and the *History of the Southern
Tang.* Supported Han Tuo-zhou's mobilization.

1204 Sent Xin Qi-ji off to the capital with an admonition to
work with Han Tuo-zhou against the Jin. Third Sung-
Jin war: Han's "northern expedition" against the Jin
began from strength, ended in disaster. Lu a supporter
throughout the conflict.

1206 Awarded the title of Earl of Wei-nan as a prowar propa-
ganda gesture. Han Tuo-zhou beheaded in palace intrigue
to appease the Jin as Sung leaders sought peace.

1208 Final retirement stipend revoked due to Lu's continued
prowar stand and criticism of the government.

1210 Lu died of old age at eighty-four sometime after the
lunar New Year.

# CHAPTER 1

# The Man Lu You

## I Life and Times

L U You was born on November 13, 1125 (the seventeenth day
of the tenth month of the year *yi-si*, being the seventh
year of the reign *xuan-he* under Emperor Hui-zong), in a boat
on the banks of the Huai River. His father, Lu Zai (d. 1147?),
a minor official from a literary family that had known better
days, was on his way to Bian-jing (Kaifeng), the Northern
Sung capital, for reassignment. Lu was given the name You
and the courtesy name Wu-guan after the poet Qin Guan
(1049–1100) whose courtesy name was Shao-you because his
mother had a dream a few days before his birth in which
she saw Qin Guan. On the basis of this maternal dream Lu
seemed destined to become a poet.

He had a stormy childhood. One year after his birth, the
Jürched Tartars captured Kaifeng and took Emperor Hui-zong
(r. 1101–26) and his son Qin-zong (r. 1126–27) along with a
host of consorts and retainers north as captives. Several years
of chaos and fighting ensued, during which time the borders
between the Jürched Jin (Golden) dynasty in the north and the
newly established Southern Sung dynasty under Emperor Gao-
zong (r. 1127–62) with its capital at Linan (Hangzhou) in
Zhejiang province became more or less permanently fixed. Lu
spent most of this time as a refugee, moving ever further south
to avoid the fighting, and it was not until he was seven or eight
that his family finally resumed a settled life in their ancestral
home in Shanyin in Shao-xing prefecture in Zhejiang.

Lu's boyhood was spent in the usual way for his age and
class—studying the classics and preparing for a bureaucratic
career. His favorite classic was the *Book of Songs* (its influence
on him will be discussed in the next chapter); but he was also

17

interested in history, which he studied under his father's guidance. From his studies of history he derived a lifelong feeling of the greatness of the Chinese nation. He also especially enjoyed reading the poets Tao Yuan-ming (365–427), Wang Wei (701–61), and Cen Shen (715–70) at this time, and, after meeting the old poet Zeng Ji (1084–1166) at age seventeen, he began the serious study of poetry.

The first great crisis of his life came at the age of nineteen or twenty when he was forced by his mother to divorce his bride of less than one year. This led to the famous "Phoenix Hairpin" incident described below. After that time he applied himself very diligently to poetry under Zeng Ji's guidance and to preparation for the official examinations. He placed first in the provincial examinations in 1153, but was removed from the lists the following year due to a conflict with Prime Minister Qin Kui's (?–1155) grandson, who took the examinations at the same time and whose grandfather expected him to be placed first on the list.

Lu finally began an undistinguished official career at thirty-three when he was made a subprefectural registrar (*zhu-bu*), a minor clerk, in Fu-zhou. He experienced several ups and downs in his early career during the time that the Sung armies battled twice with the Jin. In 1161, while Lu was at home between offices, the Sung forces under generals Liu Qi (fl. 1150) and Yu Yun-wen (1110–74) repulsed the first Jin attempt at a southern advance. Then, from 1163–64, shortly after Lu was dismissed from office for criticizing Emperor Xiao-zong's (r. 1162–89) court favorites, general Zhang Jun (?–1164) and the prowar faction convinced the new emperor to attack the north. The Sung forces were defeated at the Battle of Fu-li (in Anhui province). Lu continued to call for war against the Jin, was formally impeached and removed from office in 1167, and spent several years in rural retirement.

In 1170, at the age of forty-four, Lu was sent to far-off Sichuan, where he was to live for some eight years, including eight months in Nan-zheng (in modern Shaanxi province) on the border with the Jin expectantly awaiting a "northern expedition" and over two years in Chengdu with the poet Fan Cheng-da (1126–93), during which time his lifestyle became increasingly eccentric and reckless. His patriotic dreams of reconquest were shattered by his transfer to Chengdu, and he became increasingly interested in Daoism; poetry; and wine, women, and song. He bought a house by the Flower Washing Stream near the site of Du Fu's (712–70) Thatched Hut, styled himself "Reckless Old Man" (*Fang-weng*), and enjoyed the life of a romantic poet.

Lu's official life after his return from Sichuan was strictly anticlimactic and may be seen as merely a long preparation for his retirement and the completion of his major works. He did manage, however, to get himself impeached twice again, in 1180 and in 1189, for reckless living and being overcritical of the government.

From 1189 to his death at the age of eighty-four in the spring of 1210, he lived in retirement in Shanyin, writing poetry of an increasingly Daoist and pastoral nature. His retirement was broken only once, from 1202–03, when he went to Hangzhou to edit the *Veritable Records* of Emperors Xiao-zong and Guang-zong (r. 1189–94) and the *History of the Southern Tang* (*Nan-Tang shu*). During this time his philosophy became increasingly quietist, but he never abandoned his patriotic vision of a united empire embracing the lost northern territories. His last political act was his support of the usurper Han Tuo-zhou (?–1206) whose "northern expedition" against the Jin was launched in 1204 and ended in disastrous defeat for the Sung forces. Han was beheaded in a palace intrigue to satisfy the Jin demands, and a year later Lu lost his final retirement stipend due to his continued prowar stand and his assertion that Han had been ill-used by a cowardly Sung bureaucracy.[1]

Lu You's personality and his poetry exhibit a constant tension and oscillation between two contradictory and irreconcilable tendencies—a passion for individual freedom and an equally strong committment to public service. In Chinese terms, this tension is between the Daoist philosophy of spontaneity and enjoyment of life free from repression and social restraint, and Confucian orthodoxy with its emphasis on the subordination of the individual to the group (family and state) and the duty of the scholar to serve in public. In Lu You's personality these tendencies manifested themselves in "the play and counterplay between personalities No. 1 and No. 2,"[2] and were the complementary expressions of the outer and inner man. In Nietzsche's very useful terms, behind the Apollonian *persona* (mask) of the Confucian public servant striving mightily for and always failing to achieve "merit and fame" (*gong-ming*), there was always the Dionysian instinct to seek personal and bodily pleasures in the excitement of the chase, in drinking, and in the company of women. Lu never succeeded in completely surrendering to one or the other of these tendencies; and even though the Daoist inner vision predominated in the last decade of his life, the final pages of his poetic collection contain poems on both Daoist and patriotic themes. Most of his finest poetry may be seen as a record of his leanings in the direction of one or the other of these two powerful tendencies.

## II  *Patriotic Sentiment*

Lu You was born less than a year before the fall of northern China to an alien people, the Jürched, speakers of a Tungusic language and the ancestors of the Manchus. This conquest brought an end to what came in time to be known as the Northern Sung dynasty. The shameful fact that such "barbarians" controlled the homeland of the Chinese race dominated the thinking of Lu's father, Lu Zai, and his friends who were members of the prowar faction among the official bureaucracy of the newly established Southern Sung dynasty. Lu Zai and his friends made a great impression on the young Lu You as he studied with them in preparation for an official career. Many of them were banished to posts far away from the capital at Hangzhou (Linan) due to their views, which ran counter to Emperor Gao-zong's policy of peace (or appeasement) with the Jin (Golden) state of the Jürched. Lu remembered one of these men, Li Guang (ca. 1074–1158), in an essay written at the age of sixty-three.[3]

When Advisor Li left office and returned home I was already twenty years old. He often came to visit my father and talked with him the entire day. Every time he mentioned Qin Kui [the prime minister most responsible for the appeasement policy] he would call him Xian-yang [referring to the wicked first emperor of the Qin

dynasty] and his anger and indignation would show on his face
and in his voice.

One day he came at dawn and they ate breakfast together.
He said to my father, "I hear that when Prime Minister Zhao was
dismissed from office he was so distraught that he even burst out
crying. I will act quite differently. When the order comes down to
leave my post, I'll put on my black shoes and my linen hose [symbols
of a commoner, not an official] and walk away. How could I act like
a snivelling child?!" As he spoke these words his eyes flashed as
bright as fire and his voice resounded like a ringing bell. His heroic
and adamant attitude was very stirring and exciting.

Soon after this time Lu began his lifelong study of military
strategy and the martial arts. "Reading Martial Books at Night"
sums up his feelings at this time.[4]

> A solitary lamp illumines the frosty night,
> In deep mountains reading martial books.
> My whole life's boundless resolve:
> 4  To carry a lance and "ride before the king!"
> To die in battle: a knight's duty.
> What shame: staying with wife and child!
> Achieving merit is purely accidental,
> 8  To anticipate, mere self-deceit.
> A hungry goose calls in the marsh.
> A poor scholar cheated by the years.
> I sigh at the face in the mirror:
> 12  How preserve the lustre of youth?!

He cherished this "boundless resolve" (literally, "ten thousand
year heart" [*wan-li-xin*]) throughout his entire life and, as we
shall see in Chapter 3, this patriotic sentiment inspired some
of his most powerful poetry.

The high point of Lu's "military career," if we could call it
that, came when he spent eight months in Nan-zheng on the
border between the Sung and the Jin as advisor to the Chief
Pacification Officer Wang Yan (1138–1218). His hopes for a
reconquest of the northern lands were very high at this time,
and he offered his advice to Wang Yan, but it was never
followed. The following poem, "Travelling South of the Mountain," was written shortly after he arrived in Nan-zheng after a

difficult mountain journey from Kui-zhou. It expresses quite
well his awareness of the strategic importance of the Shaan-nan
area (modern southern Shaanxi where Nan-zheng was located)
and his strategy of attacking from a position of strength in this
"Land Within the Passes."[5]

> Already three days I've travelled south of the mountain.
> The great road like a string stretches east to west.
> Level streams, rich fields, gaze cannot exhaust.
> 4 Wheat fields grass green, mulberries lush dark.
> In the land of Han-Qin spirit and customs are brave,
> Sides are chosen to play at swings and kick ball.
> Clover grows to the clouds—stout the horses' legs.
> 8 Willows line the roads—loud the carriages' rumble.
> From ancient times for generations a place of rise
>      and fall.
> Look up: rivers, mountains, ever like before.
> Cold clouds lower around the General's Altar.
> 12 Spring sun sets before the Prime Minister's Temple.
> Nation has lost Central Plains full fifty years.
> Troops move out from Jiang-Huai, are not easily
>      swallowed.
> To see gongs and drums followed throughout the land,
> 16 Make this Land Within the Passes serve our solid stand!

There was an altar south of Nan-zheng city said to have been
the place where the Han Emperor Gao-zu (r. 206–194 B.C.)
made Han Xin (fl. 2nd cent. B.C.) a great general. A memorial
temple to Zhu-ge Liang (181–234), the prime minister of the
Shu-Han kingdom during the Three Kingdoms period, was also
located nearby.[6] "Land Within the Passes" (guan-zhong) was
the ancient name for present day Shaanxi, the original area of
the Qin dynasty and of great strategic importance throughout
Chinese history.

Lu's hopes for reconquest in Nan-zheng were shattered, but
he never gave up the idea that one day the Chinese troops
would march north and defeat the Jin armies. This fervent
belief was the basis for his support of the otherwise unsavory
political usurper Han Tuo-zhou whose "northern expedition"
against the Jin ended in disaster in 1206 when Lu was nearly
eighty. He did not regret his support of Han even though it

caused him to be deprived of his final retirement stipend at eighty-two. He blamed the Sung defeat on the half-hearted support of the court and the cowardice of the ruling elite. The final poem in his collection, one every Chinese schoolchild knows by heart, is entitled "For My Sons" and expresses his last patriotic wish.[7]

> Dying away, always knew myriad affairs were empty;
> Only sad I never saw the Nine Islands united.
> The day our king's troops pacify the Central Plains,
> At family sacrifices don't forget to tell your father!

### III   *Romantic Legend*

There are many romantic stories about Lu You's amorous exploits, but none of these episodes has more exercised the minds of later writers than the tragic story of his first marriage and his romantic devotion to his first love. Not long after his nineteenth or twentieth birthday, Lu married his childhood sweetheart and cousin, Tang Wan, who was his mother's brother's daughter. He had known her from about the age of four, and her family had lived near his in Shanyin for many years before that time. She should have been an ideal match both for Lu and his family, but for some still unexplained reason Lu's mother refused to accept her. She first forced the young couple to separate and finally forced Lu to divorce his bride of less than one year. This tragic dénouement had a considerable influence on Lu's poetry and personality and also led to a romantic legend known as the "Phoenix Hairpin" (*chai-tou-feng*) incident from the title of a lyric meter (*ci*) Lu is said to have written when he met Tang Wan some ten years later.

The most reliable and complete version of the story is to be found in the *Wild Words from Eastern Qi* (*Qi-dong ye-yu*) of Zhou Mi (1232–1308). It reads in part as follows:[8]

Lu Wu-guan first married Miss Tang, the daughter of [Tang] Hong and his mother's niece. The couple got on very well, but did not have the approval of the mother.

[The divorce is described.]

Tang [Wan] was later remarried to a distant relative of the same county, one [Zhao] Shi-cheng. [They: Lu and the Zhaos] often went on outings in the spring, and they met once at the Shen family garden south of the Yu-ji Monastery. Tang [Wan] asked Zhao to have some sweetmeats and wine sent over to Lu. Lu was sadly moved for some time, and then he composed the lyric meter 'Phoenix Hairpin' for the occasion and wrote it on the garden wall:

> Pink powdered arm,
> Yellow wine jar,
> Whole city in spring colors, willows
>     by the palace wall.
> East wind cruel,
> Happy times rare,
> A breast full of sad feelings:
> Many years of separation.
> 8  Wrong! Wrong! Wrong!
>
> Spring like before,
> You're thin for nothing,
> Mermaid's silk soaked with tear
>     streaks red and wet.
> 4  Peach blossoms fall,
> Deserted pool and pavilion.
> The mountain pledge still remains,
> But a brocade letter is hard to send.
> 8  No! No! No!

This occurred in the *yi-hai* year of the *shao-xing* reign period [1155]. Miss Tang died shortly after that time. . . .

As an old man [Lu] lived at Three Mountains (*san-shan*) near Mirror Lake. In his later years every time he went into the city he would have to go up to the monastery and look around; it was emotionally unbearable. Another two quatrains follow:

Dream shattered, fragrance gone, forty long years.
Shen's Garden willow has aged, scatters no floss.
When this body has turned to earth under Mount Ji,
My tears will still mourn her lingering traces.

As sun sets, on the wall a painted horn sounds mournfully.
Shen's Garden cannot restore its former pools and terraces.
My heart aches under the bridge by spring ripples green:
To think the frightened swan's image was once mirrored here!

[Zhou says these poems were written in 1199, when Lu was seventy-four, and then concludes with two more quatrains written in 1205 at eighty. I reproduce only one here.]

> The small path south of the city is once more in spring;
> I only see plum blossoms, do not see her:
> Jade bones long become earth under the stream.
> Ink traces still locked into the dust of the wall.

The Shen Garden later belonged to Mr. Xu, and still later was the home of one Wang Zhi-dao.

Lu often returned to Shen's Garden to relive his memories of Tang Wan and their ill-fated romance, and he wrote many other poems in memory of her throughout his life.

This story, repeated and embellished by later writers, also became the subject of a Peking opera entitled "Phoenix Hairpin," which is still occasionally performed on the Chinese stage.[9]

We also know that Lu had a number of romantic liaisons in Sichuan and that he brought a concubine, neé Yang, back with him when he returned to the east in 1178. She bore him at least one child, a daughter nicknamed "girly" (*nü-nü*) who died of illness at the age of one. Lu left a son, Zi Bu, his fifth (?), in Sichuan when he came east, and Professor Wolfram Eberhard has suggested to me, I think quite rightly, that "he had a liaison there from which a boy resulted, but not from Yang, the concubine, because she lived with him," and he would have taken any son by her home with him to Shanyin.[10] The word Lu most often used to describe his lifestyle in Sichuan after 1172 was *kuang*, which may be translated as "crazy," "wild," "mad(cap)," and "eccentric"; it also often simply indicates an unusually rich love life.[11]

It was during this time that he styled himself the "Reckless Old Man" (*Fang-weng*) and enjoyed nothing more than drinking, gambling, and frequenting the courtesans' quarters. The poem given on page 54 below gives a vivid picture of his happy days in Sichuan.

There is one aspect of the Lu You legend that he wrote about often enough himself for me to believe it. It is the kind of story the Chinese love to tell in their episodic novels of romantic

26                                                        LU YOU

heroes, and it describes how one autumn afternoon while hunting
with a party of soldiers in the mountains near Nan-zheng he
killed a tiger with a lance. According to his own later account of
the event, when they first encountered the tiger most of the men
in his party froze stiff with fear; but he spurred his horse
on toward the place where the tiger's growls had been heard.
Just as the tiger ran out of the brush and straight at him, he
braced himself in the saddle and thrust out his long lance, pierc-
ing the tiger's heart with a blow that splattered both himself
and his horse with hot blood. The following lines from a poem
written several years after the event are about the best that he
wrote on this unforgettable adventure. The long title—"On the
night of the twenty-fourth of the tenth month I dreamed I was
travelling on the Nan-zheng road; I woke up with a start and
wrote this poem. The time was already five in the morning"—
is typical of Lu's style.[12]

Fiercely glares the north mountain tiger,
Without number the people he's eaten.
For orphans and widows no revenge is taken.
4  Sun sets, wind rises, travellers are frightened.
I rolled up my sleeves as I heard
His great growl from a hundred paces.
Strong and straight, lance thrust forward;
tiger stood like a man,
8  Growling rent the green ravine, blood
gushed like a stream!
My fellow riders, thirty, all men of Qin,
Faces pale, spirits shaken, emptily looked around.
. . .
Now today, weak and sick, I lie in bed,
12  Beat my fists, longing still to prepare a
border campaign.
Who says southern men don't understand weapons?
Of old Chu's three families annihilated Qin!

Lu was himself a southern man whose ancestors originally
came from the state of Chu and he loved to recall that the
armies of Liu Bang, the first emperor of the Han dynasty, were
largely made up of peasants from Chu.

Another aspect of Lu's passionate temperament was expressed in his powerful and beautiful calligraphy. Often when he was feeling particularly depressed because of the failure of the Sung rulers to attack the Jin, or because of his own poor showing in office, he would turn to wine and calligraphy in order to forget his restless sorrow. "Calligraphy Song" describes this quite well.[13]

> I ruin my family brewing three thousand gallons
>     of wine.
> I've ten thousand gallons of restless sorrow:
>     wine can't touch it.
> This morning my drunken eyes are as bright as
>     lightning over the cliffs.
> 4 Take up my brush and look around: Heaven and Earth
>     are so narrow!
> Suddenly my sweeping stroke is beyond my control:
> Wind and clouds fill my breast, Heaven lends me
>     strength!
> Sacred dragons fight in the meadow, dark and rank
>     their vapors!
> 8 Weird ghosts push up the mountains, blacken the
>     bright moon!
> By now, the sorrow in my breast completely driven out,
> I slap the bed, give a loud shout, wildly throw down
>     my cap!
> Neither the fine paper of Wu nor the silk of Shu
>     are good enough:
> 12 I *must* paint the nine foot wall of my high hall!

Line three contains an allusion to Wang Rong (234–305), one of the Seven Sages of the Bamboo Grove, eccentrics of the late Han and early Three Kingdoms periods, who was said to have been able to look into the sun without becoming dizzy and whose eyes were said to flash like lightning.[14] Lu often uses this image to describe his own drunken visage. Lines five to eight describe the force of his calligraphy in cosmic terms. The "sacred dragons" (*shen-long*) are mentioned in the *Book of Changes*, one of Lu's favorite books, under the hexagram number two, *kun*, "Earth or Receptive": "Dragons fight in the meadow. Their blood is black and yellow."[15]

Outwardly, then, Lu was a man of great passion and a man who loved action and adventure, a man of great energy who enjoyed very much the delights of the body and the pleasures of life. His great love of life even led him inwardly to long for and dream of the possibility of immortality.

## IV  Daoism and the Occult

Lu You's interest in Daoism, both in its lofty philosophical aspect as represented in the *Lao Zi* and *Zhuang Zi* and in its popular aspect as a search for physical immortality, goes back at least to his early thirties and probably earlier. A later chapter will be devoted to his Daoist and alchemical poems. Here I merely wish to mention a few incidents in his life that demonstrate his continuing belief in what are today called "occult phenomena."

In the spring of 1166, at the age of forty, Lu met an "extraordinary man" (*yi-ren*), an immortal or adept, on West Mountain in Nan-chang (in modern Jiangxi province) and received from him the "pine-chrysanthemum method [of immortality] of Si-ma Zi-wei."[16] This experience convinced him to keep on studying Daoism and searching for elixirs of immortality. At this time he also visited many famous Daoist temples, such as the Yu-long Wan-shou Guan ("Longevity Temple") in the Jiangxi area, to discuss the Way with the monks or to borrow Daoist books.

The following year Lu was impeached from office for the first of three times and went home to live in rural seclusion and forced retirement. Before the age of sixty-four, it was always at times like these that he turned his mind away from external events and inward toward philosophical and religious speculation. The poem entitled "Feelings on Reading Recluse Books at Night" describes well his state of mind during such phases of his life.[17]

> My whole life-will yearns for White Cloud Realms.
> Bowing and scraping in the human world,
> I only injure myself.
> Tired crane broken and ruined, yet hopes for food.

4 Cold tortoise, wrinkled and withdrawn, still supports
     the bed.
  Diligently explore the *Vast Treasure,* seeking wondrous
     formulae.
  Abundantly pick "green essence," testing arcane
     prescriptions.
  I've ever despised scrawny "immortals" aging in
     mountain marsh.
8 Want to make them raise their heads, watch me
     soar aloft!

"White Cloud Realms" (*bai-yun-xiang*) are mentioned in *Zhuang Zi,* Chapter twelve, as the land of the immortals where the heavenly emperor dwells. The crane and the tortoise are common Daoist symbols, but are mentioned here in an ambiguous manner. The "tired crane" (*juan-he*) may refer to Lu himself and the "food" (*liao*) it still desires may be the Daoist elixirs mentioned in the last four lines of the poem. There may, however, also be a pun intended on the term *he-liao,* "crane food," which was a common euphemism for an official salary. In that case, Lu may be still hoping for an official appointment, as no doubt he was at this time. The tortoise serves both as a conventional Daoist symbol of longevity, referring here to Lu's search for elixirs, and also to set the scene in his bedroom study, since bed legs rested on tortoise-shaped feet in the Zhejiang area (giving rise to the common expression "tortoise bed" [*gui-chuang*]). Lines three and four, then, may refer either to seeking office in retirement in spite of its dangers or to searching for Daoist alchemical knowledge and immortality.

The "*Vast Treasure*" (*hong-bao*) is one title given to a work by the Han dynasty Daoist scholar Liu An (ca. 178–122 B.C.), Prince of Huai-nan. According to his biographers, he had a book that described the secret alchemical art of turning cinnabar into gold, as well as the secret of immortality. Just before he became an immortal (*xian-qu*), he gave a potion to some chickens and dogs and they were all miraculously able to fly, to "soar aloft" as in the last line of this poem. "Green essence" (*qing-jing*), also known as "green essence gruel" (*fan*) and "southern candle grass" (*nan-zhu-cao*) among other names, is a plant common in the Hangzhou area of Zhejiang that the Daoists believed conferred immortality upon the eater.

The last two lines seem to express Lu's dislike and distrust of pseudoadepts and false "immortals" who grow old and die, and his fervent wish to become a true immortal or transcendent (*xian*) and "soar aloft" (*fei-xiang*), perhaps on the back of a crane, like the feathered immortals of Han dynasty iconography.[18]

Several years later, when Lu travelled from Nan-zheng to Chengdu after his hopes for an immediate northern expedition were shattered, he visited the famous Green Wall Mountain (*qing-cheng-shan*) in modern Sichuan, Guan-*xian*, a Daoist stronghold, where he lodged at the Zhang-ren Guan. He met another eccentric old man by the name of Shang-guan Dao-ren ("Man of the Way from Shang-guan") who made a great impression on him.[19] The old man lived in a tree, refused to eat cooked food, and rarely talked with or listened to other people. Lu felt himself quite fortunate that the old man talked with him concerning the arts of achieving longevity; he advised Lu that longevity was possible for everyone to obtain, but that it takes great perseverence and discipline. Lu later wrote several poems about this remarkable old man. The following poem is a typical example.[20]

I recently travelled to Green Wall. I often wandered with Shang-guan Dao-weng. In the heat I suddenly think of him.

> Years past I often travelled to Zhang-ren Temple.
> Shang-guan at eighty was like a little babe.
> Said himself in youth his deafness could not be
>     cured.
> 4  With pine nuts and magic fungus, he never hungered.
> Kowtowing I got no answer, he merely smiled broadly.
> The countenance of a Holy Man surely does instruct.
> I'd heard studying the Way requires essential thought
> 8  That must not stop an instant in a lifetime.
> Although the Master was deadly quiet, his meaning
>     could be known:
> "The reason the lamb was lost—too many forks in
>     the road."
> Go away and wander with him; it's really not too late.

12  Our staffs together, straddle the seas, seek our own
season of peace.

After his retirement at sixty-four, Lu began the work of
refining the Great Elixir, to be examined in detail below, and
his political ideals became more and more modelled on the
Daoist vision of utopia where people live content with simplicity
and hard work on the land and where there are no wars and no
famines. "Mount Ji Peasants" presents one of the finest poetic
statements of this ideal.[21]

> Land of the Flower Clan's
> A fit place for me to live.
> People of the Contented Clan
> 4  Fit to be my friends.
> Eyes like cliff lightning, looking upon no one.
> Belly like a wine bag, sated with wine.
> Duke Zhou's rites and music, silenced, not passed on.
> 8  Si-Ma's martial laws lost for so long.
> Today at least Shen Nong's science still remains.
> Lean on the plow and learn yet from your rustic elders:
> Wear coarse silk and heavy cloth to resist winter,
> 12  Hull your own yellow sorgum and black millet,
> Cut leeks from your own garden, sweeter than meat,
> Dip new wine, thick as gruel, from festival pots.
> How can we achieve abundant harvests for all the world,
> 16  Age and die and never see beacon fires of war?
> Cut out profit and fame, never speak of them again!
> For generations, my sons, work as Mount Ji peasants!

The first two lines refer to a primitive community mentioned
in the Daoist classic *Lie Zi*: "The Yellow Ancestor (*huang-di*)
was sleeping in the daytime and travelled in a dream to the
country of the Flower Clan (*hua-xu-shi zhi guo*). There were no
generals or leaders in their country; everything was perfectly
natural. Their people had no cravings or desires; everything was
quite natural."[22] The next two lines refer to another similar
community mentioned in an obscure Sung dynasty book of
Daoist mythology and legend: the people "relished their food,
enjoyed their customs, were content with their dwellings, and
took care of their livelihood. Their bodies had activity and

labor, but their minds knew neither likes nor dislikes. They
died of old age without ever visiting back and forth."[23] Lines
seven and eight refer to the decline of morality and military
strategy, a strange combination, but typically linked in Lu's
mind, since the golden age of the Duke of Zhou, Confucius'
reputed mentor, and the legendary military strategist Si-ma
Rang-ju. Fortunately, Lu writes in the next few lines, agriculture,
the "science" (xue) of the demigod Shen Nong, still remains to
bring stability to social life if rightly practiced and understood.
If only people were content with the simple life and did not
stretch out their desires for profit and fame.

Sometime in his late sixties Lu began to practice Daoist style
meditation with great seriousness, and at the age of eighty-one,
at the same time that he was applauding the abortive northern
expedition of Han Tuo-zhou, he achieved what must have been
the high point of his meditation practices when he had a vision
of light or an illumination—a realization of inner power that
gave him a strong feeling of transcendence. The title of the
poem he wrote on that occasion tells the story.[24]

On the night of the twenty-seventh of the eleventh month [1206],
I put on my clothes and sat up [meditating, zuo]. A spiritual light
[shen-guang] flashed forth from the corners of my eyes like the
morning sun. The entire room was illuminated [ming]. I wrote this
poem to record the event.

> Spirit-house without thought, heel-breath stilled,
> Eyes flash divine light, illumine window and door.
> Great hat, long sword, finally no more.
> 4  Small house, tiny garden, just now returned.
> Worries, troubles pass before: all dream stuff;
> Merit, fame forever opposed to heart.
> Three peaks, two mansions, smoke-dust quieted;
> 8  Now I'll wear oak leaf clothes under frosty sky.

"Spirit-house" (ling-fu) is a Daoist term for the mind taken
from the Zhuang Zi, Chapter five. "Heal-breath" (zhong-xi)
refers to the practice of extremely deep breathing said by
Zhuang Zi to be characteristic of the Daoist True Man. "The
True Man breathes with his heels; the mass of men breathe
with their throats."[25] The "great hat" (da-guan) of lines three

d four refers to his Confucian official's hat, and the lines
press rejection of official life and return to his rural home.
ne seven means that he is quiet both in his mind and in his
aterial life and is ready to become a mountain dwelling im-
ortal, to become one with nature. "Three peaks" (*san-feng*)
nvolves a complex allusion that refers to his quiet heart. The
'three peaks" are those of Hua-shan ("Flowery Mountain") in
Shaanxi, one of the five sacred mountains of China. The *Zhuang
Zi*, Chapter thirty-three, relates that Sung Jian and Yin Wen,
pacifists who belived in purity of heart, "fashioned caps in the
shape of Mount Hua to be their mark of distinction."[26] Com-
mentators say that the expression "Mount Hua cap" (*hua-shan
zhi guan*) refers to one whose heart is quiet. The "two mansions"
(*er-shi*) is an allusion to another story from the *Zhuang Zi*,
Chapter twenty-eight, concerning Yuan Xian, a disciple of Confucius famous for his indifference to poverty. He lived in a tiny
thatched house that "had a broken door made of woven brambles
and branches of mulberry for the doorposts; jars with the bottoms
out, hung with pieces of coarse cloth for protection from the
weather, served as windows for its *two rooms*. The roof leaked
and the floor was damp, but Yuan Xian sat up in dignified
manner, played his lute, and sang."[27] When Confucius' most
affluent disciple, Zi-gong, commisserated with Yuan about his
distress, Yuan answered, "I have heard that if one lacks wealth,
that is called poverty; and if one studies but cannot put into
practice what he has learned, that is called distress. *I am poor,
but I am not in distress!*"[28] The last line describes the hermit
going off to dwell in nature wearing clothing made from "oak
leaf" (*xie-ye*); this too may be an allusion.

From the frequency with which he writes of contentment
with a simple life of poverty in his last ten years, he may have
lived in rather straightened circumstances during that time. In
his most active years, however, it is quite unlikely that he
was ever really poverty-stricken. In his youth he travelled
extensively before he had an official appointment. He often
enjoyed wine and entertainments that were far from in-
expensive. In spite of the fact that he did not receive formal
military training, he learned horseback riding quite well and
probably rented or owned a horse or horses, also an expensive

business. He also had a wife and concubine and perhaps as
many as ten children. It is obvious that he could not pay for
all of these things out of his official salary from the many
minor posts he held. His most critical biographer, Zhu Dong-ren,
discusses this question at length, pointing out that Lu had a
good income from his landholdings, which were worked by
tenant farmers, and concluding that his often-stated contentment with poverty was merely a poetic cliche.[29] He was a proud
man and the image of an impoverished old Daoist sage was
one that he very much liked to present in his later years.

Although he may not have been as poor as he liked to
imply, there can be no doubt that in his old age he was sus-
tained by his faith in Daoism. In the autumn of 1209, at the
age of eighty-three, he was sick in bed for seventy days with
some sort of pulmonary illness. Although the disease subsided
at times, he never really recovered from it, but grew steadily
weaker. Sometimes he could walk a short distance with someone
helping him, but then he would have to rest for several minutes.
In bed he continued to read the *Zhuang Zi* and the poetry of
Tao Yuan-ming. Like a true Daoist, he loked upon his approaching death as just another great change in life, one of many he
had endured, and he reminded himself that "life and death
equal day and night." Finally, as death grew ever nearer, he
seems to have felt like C.G. Jung's "archetype of *the old man
who has seen enough*," and had Jung's same "feeling of kinship
with all things."[30] He wrote of his death as a "true return"
(*zhen-gui*) with "no thoughts" (*wu-nian*) of ego separation
from the ten thousand things of creation. The title of the following poem, written on his deathbed, is "Moaning and Groaning."[31]

Moan and groan half a year behind wattle door;
Life force barely remains, breath and vigor wane.
My fate could not escape coarse grains.
4 Living poor, luckily used to rough bedding.
Muddy or clear now briefly distinguish worthy from sage.
Yesterday or today, who can reason right from wrong?
Remember well one piece of honest advice:
8 Have no thoughts, that's true return!

Lu You the Daoist, like his Master Zhuang Zhou, would surely answer that the solution to the problem of "right and wrong" (*shi-fei*) is to give up trying to reason it out and to transcend the petty distinctions of the world. As the *Zhuang Zi* states,[32]

When the Way relies on little accomplishments and words rely on vain show, then we have the rights and wrongs of the Confucians and the Mo-ists. What one calls right the other calls wrong; what one calls wrong the other calls right. But if we want to right their wrongs and wrong their rights, then the best thing to use is clarity [*ming*]. . . . So the sage harmonizes with both right and wrong and rests in Heaven the Equalizer. . . . Those who discriminate fail to see. . . . Harmonize them all [i.e., all distinctions] with the Heavenly Equality, *leave them to their endless changes*, and so live out your years. . . . Forget the years; *forget distinctions*. Leap into the boundless and make it your home.

CHAPTER 2

# From Realism to Transcendence: The Origin and Development of Lu You's Poetic Style

AT first glance, the sheer quantity of Lu You's poetic production is staggering. His poetry collection, the *Jian-nan shi-gao*, has eighty-five chapters and contains some 9,220 poems; add to that the two chapters of poems in his supplementary collection, the *Fang-weng Yi-gao*, and the total amounts to more than ten thousand poems! According to the *Colophon to Jian-nan shi-gao*, written by his son Zi-yu in 1221, Lu himself put together the first *shi-gao* in twenty chapters and personally supervised the editing of the second edition in forty chapters, called the *Jian-nan-shi xu-gao*. The remaining chapters were assembled on the basis of Lu's wishes by Zi-yu. As Zi-yu wrote, Lu "never for one day forgot Shu (Sichuan)," and thus his collection was given the name of an area in Sichuan near Chengdu where he spent so many enjoyable days.[1]

Critics ancient and modern have followed Lu's own evaluations in dividing his stylistic development into early, middle, and late periods. In his many poems describing these stages, Lu was quite consistent and definite about them. I shall first present several poems in which Lu describes his poetic progress, and then discuss the major characteristics of each period before going on to describe the way in which Lu admired and learned from particular poets whose works made up his poetic heritage.

The first poem, "Reflections on Reading My *Poetic Collection*," was written at the age of sixty-seven and delineates rather fully his three poetic periods.[2]

> Studying poetry long ago I gained nothing from it,
> Couldn't avoid begging scraps from other people.

Knew well at heart my verse lacked force and vigor,
4   Was shame-faced at my undeserved empty name.
    At forty following the army, stationed at Nan-zheng;
    Night into day drunkenly revelled with the troops.
    Played polo, pounding the field for a thousand yards.
8   Reviewed cavalry, lining them up three thousand strong.
    By colorful lamps wildly gambled, shouts filling the hall.
    Bejeweled hairpieces, seductively dancing, shimmered
        around the table.
    Frantically strumming lute strings: wild icy hail.
12  Rhythmically beating drum skins: angry windy rain.
    Master poets' Secret Art suddenly appeared before me,
    I understood Qu and Jia with utmost lucid clarity!
    Heavenly Loom's Cloud Brocade *must be created by me!*
16  Subtle Art of cutting material is not in knife or rule!
    The world's highest talent certainly isn't lacking:
    Miss by a hair's breadth, you're worlds off the mark!
    Fang-weng aging, dying, hardly worth discussing;
20  Xi Kang's song cut short still provokes sadness.

The first four lines refer to the ten years he spent studying
with Zeng Ji and imitating earlier poets in the fashion of the
Jiangxi School, to be discussed below, and indicate his later
dissatisfaction with his early poetry. He discarded nearly all of
the poems from those early years. The next eight lines refer to
his romantic experiences on the Sung-Jin border in Nan-zheng,
experiences that he felt led him to the realization that true
poetry could only be created by his own individual creative
imagination working upon the materials of his real life experiences. He characteristically described this realization in the
language of religious mysticism as an "awakening" (*wu*). The
"Master poets' Secret Art" is literally "the poet's *Samadhi*"
(*shi-jia san-mei*), a Buddhist term that means a very high state
of meditation in which one experiences "perfect absorption of
thought into the one object of meditation."[3] Qu and Jia are
Qu Yuan (4th century B.C., see below) and Jia Yi (201–169 B.C.),
the latter a Han dynasty rhyme-prose (*fu*) writer, both of whom
Lu learned from during his middle period. Jia Yi is a particularly
apt person for Lu to compare himself with as he looked back
on his middle period in Sichuan, since Jia too had been exiled
from court and, while preoccupied with the nation's troubles,

tried to console himself with the Daoist philosophy of the *Zhuang Zi*. The "Heavenly Loom" (*tian-ji*) could also be translated as the "Heavenly Secret," the "Mystery of Creation," or the "Mystery of the Universe."[4] The "Cloud Brocade" (*yun-jin*) refers both to the color of morning clouds and to the clothing of unearthly beauty worn by the gods.

The poem concludes with two lines on the great difficulty involved in perfecting one's talents and two lines lamenting the fact that the great poetic secret of individual creation probably cannot be passed on. Xi Kang (223–62), one of the Seven Sages of the Bamboo Grove that Lu often alludes to, was a Daoist who wrote an essay on nurturing life and seeking immortality. He failed in his quest, however, and was executed for attempting to defend a friend from false accusations. He was also a famous lutanist and master of a song called the *Guang-ling-san*; just before his execution he is said to have played his lute, wept, and remarked that "from this time on the *Guang-ling-san* will be cut off!"[5] Lu felt that creativity was an individual and intuitive act of imagination and in this allusion he lamented the fact that he could not pass on his Secret Art.

"Roaming the Hills Writing Poems at the Beginning of Autumn" was written at the age of seventy-seven and once more delineates his three poetic periods, concluding with the feeling that his final period was his best.[6]

> In youth beginning to study poetry,
> Reckless ambition copied *Feng* and *Ya*.
> In middle years beset with troubles,
> 4  Wanted then to follow Qu and Jia.
> How'd I know, so rough and unskilled,
> That I'd achieve mere dregs and dross?
> Entering the sea not nearly deep enough,
> 8  Fine pearls hardly filled one hand.
> With age comes slight improvement;
> When inspired poems pour forth.
> Still able to encourage later students,
> 12  Yellow River swallows the Great Marsh!

The first eight lines describe his first two periods in a manner similar to the previous poem, but show Lu then to be dissatisfied

with his middle period works. All that outpouring of anger and
anxiety, all those "tears of national worry" (*you-guo-lei*) and
passionate expressions of desire for "merit and fame" (*gong-ming*) now seem to him to amount to very few "real pearls"
(*zhu-ji*), fine poems often being referred to as "a belly full of
pearls" (*man-fu zhu-ji*). The last four lines describe his later
poetry as an improvement over that of his earlier periods. At
this point he felt himself to be writing naturally, spontaneously,
and calmly in response to any situation or event that moved
him, and his mastery of formal technical skills had reached a
point where he no longer had to work at it. He felt capable
of pouring forth his feelings at any particular time and place
"when inspired" (*yu-xing*). *Xing* is translated "inspired-inspi-ration" because it generally means "incitement-stimulus-interest"
or their verbal equivalent and was used from most ancient times
as a technical term in Chinese literary criticism.

The last poem to be discussed in this context, "For Zi-yu,"
was written at the age of eighty-three for his son.[7] Besides
reiterating his dissatisfaction with the poetry of his first two
periods, the poem also emphasizes his great love of poetry and
his abiding belief that truly great poetry must be based on real
life experiences and represent something more than mastery of
the prosodic rules and verbal dexterity.

> When I began to study poetry,
> Only wanted to perfect decorative form.
> Middle age brought slight awakening,
> 4 Gradual search for grander vision.
> Strange wondrous images jutted out
> Like rocks washed by thunderous torrent!
> So lofty is Li and Du's edifice;
> 8 Always regret I lack their talent.
> Yuan and Bo leaned at their gate;
> Wen and Li merit no comment.
> Carrying a tripod with your brush,
> 12 Still misses the poets' Secret.
> Poetry's one of the Fine Arts;
> How can they cheapen her so!
> If you truly want to learn poetry,
> 16 Its mastery lies beyond prosody.

Although he had written earlier that he "gained nothing from it," actually in his studies with Zeng Ji he learned to "perfect" (*gong*) the elegance and adornment of form, the "decorative form" (*cao-hui*) characteristic of the Jiangxi School. In his "middle years" (*zhong-nian*) his poetry began to change and become more characteristically "heroic and unrestrained" (*hao-si*) as a result of his travels, his military experiences, and his reading of Du Fu (712–70), Li Bo (701–62), and Cen Shen. He paid high tribute here to Li Bo and Du Fu in lines seven and eight, putting himself in the position of their disciple and them in the position of Confucius himself by alluding to a passage from the *Analects of Confucius*. Once someone at court said that Confucius's disciple Zi-gong was a better man than the master. Zi-gong replied, "Let us take as our comparison the wall round a building. My wall only reaches to the level of a man's shoulder, and it is easy enough to peep over it and see the good points of the house on the other side. But our Master's wall (my "edifice") rises many times a man's height, and no one who is not let in by the gate can know the beauty and wealth of the palace that...lies within."[8] Lu continues the image in the next two lines, criticising later poets who thought that they were following Li Bo and Du Fu. Yuan Zhen (779–831) and Bo Ju-yi (772–846) were poets of the Middle Tang period who followed the single aspect of Du Fu's poetry concerned with realistic social criticism. To that extent they only "leaned at his gate" (*yi-men*) and never made it into his "lofty edifice" to share the fullness of his poetic secrets. Wen Ting-yun (813?–70) supposedly followed Li Bo in the writing of "lyric meters" (*ci*), but his poetry may be regarded as the very perfection of "decorative form" without genuine content. Li Shang-yin (813?–58) was, like Wen, a poet of the Late Tang period, and he too consciously imitated Du Fu, but in a manner quite the opposite of Yuan and Bo. He studied Du Fu in order to perfect the elegance and technical mastery of the Regulated Verse form (*lü-shi*) of Du Fu's later years. As we shall see, Lu heartily disliked the Late Tang poets, feeling that they were responsible for the complete eclipse of the *Book of Songs* and the *Chu Elegies* traditions of social criticism in poetry; here he merely wrote that they deserve no comment in comparison to Li and Du.

The last six lines argue that good poetry is not necessarily a literary tour de force to be likened to carrying a heavy bronze tripod on the end of a thin bamboo writing brush. Such empty show will never "achieve the poets' Secret" (*zao san-mei*). Poetry is one of the "Fine Arts," literally, one of the "Six Arts" (*liu-yi*) of classical antiquity whose correct practice would assure peace and harmony in the state through the creation of goodness and morality. Thus the mastery of true poetry "lies beyond prosody" (*gong-fu zai shi-wai*), beyond mere technical excellence of form. In criticising Yuan and Bo for being too concerned with realism and social criticism and Wen and Li for erring in the direction of excessive elegance of form, Lu seems to be calling for a poetry that is at once sincere and realistic in content, like the *Book of Songs, and* imaginative and beautiful in form, like the *Chu Elegies.* Of later poets, according to Lu, only Li Bo and Du Fu have lived up to the great Chinese poetic tradition.

Thus, Lu's poetic development may be divided into three stylistic periods, remembering, of course, that the transition from one to another was gradual over time and not abrupt and definite. In general, though, the early period comprises the poetry written from the age of sixteen or seventeen to forty-five, some twenty-nine years that are represented in the *Jian-nan shi-gao* chapters one and two and include only some 230 poems. Although these poems should represent his period of imitation and "perfection of decorative form," most of the finely polished lines of regulated verse occur in poems whose overall impact is typically forceful and vigorous and whose themes are quite often serious and imbued with social concern.

The middle period includes the poetry written from age forty-five to sixty-four, some nineteen years spent travelling to and from Sichuan, living in Chengdu and many other places, and ending in his impeachment and retirement. It includes some 2,500 poems in chapters two to twenty-one of his *shi-gao,* all but the final twenty-five poems in chapter twenty-one chosen for inclusion by Lu himself. The verse of this period is generally expansive and unrestrained, full of passionate and often angry expressions of personal and national ambition, the desire to make an illustrious career and to establish "merit and fame" (*gong-ming*) through service to the country, especially service leading to a military reconquest of the lost northern territories. When that dream exploded and he was transferred to Chengdu, he became even more unrestrained and eccentric in his personal behavior, and his poetry continued to be highly individualistic and imaginative. He buried his feelings of sadness and personal frustration in drinking and reckless living, and expressed his great resentment against the appeasement party, the emperor, and all those responsible for the decision not to fight the Jürched in heroic-patriotic poetry that we shall examine in detail below. He was primarily influenced by Qu Yuan, Du Fu, Li Bo, and Cen Shen at this time.

Lu's late period includes the poetry written from the age of sixty-four to his death at eighty-four, about twenty very creative years that are represented by some 6,500 poems in chapters twenty-one to eighty-five of his collection. More than two-thirds of his poetic production was written after the age of sixty-four, during which time he came gradually to accept, however grudgingly, the fact that he was first, last, and always a poet, and that his fame would rest on the reputation of his poetry. Although there are still many poems written in the heroic mode, the main themes of his last period are Daoist philosophy, including alchemy and meditation, landscape (*shan-shui*) poetry, and pastoral (*tian-yuan*) poetry which also concerned his daily life in rural Zhejiang. While still praising the poetry of Li Bo and Du Fu, he more frequently mentioned Tao Yuan-ming and Mei Yao-chen (1002–60) as his own poetry approached a stage of "calm" (*ping-dan*) similar to theirs.

## I   *Jiangxi School, Zeng Ji and*
## *Lu's Discovery of the Tang Poets*

The early period of the Southern Sung dynasty was an age of minor poets, and the Jiangxi School is the name given by later critics to a group of minor poets of that time. Lü Ju-ren (or Ben-zhong, 1137–81) was one of them who once drew up a list of some twenty-six of his contemporaries who were assiduous imitators of the Northern Sung poet Huang Ting-jian (1045–1105), himself an imitator of Du Fu and the poets of the High Tang period. Huang was a native of Jiangxi Province, and thus the name of the group of his followers. Lü Ju-ren, like all the others of the school, tried to follow Huang, but was not very successful at it. As Professor Yoshikawa Kojiro puts it, Huang "had a fondness for the little details of daily life, and observed them closely because he hoped to discover within them some larger meaning. But Lü Ju-ren, in attempting to carry on Huang's style, took over his taste for detail without any of the deeper significance, and his poetry succeeds in being merely miniature."[9] The Jiangxi School, however had great influence on later Sung poetry; Liu Ke-zhuang (1187–1269) and Yang Wan-li (1124–1206) first learned poetry from it, as did Lu You.

Lu was influenced by the Jiangxi style through his seven years of study with Zeng Ji, a well-known adherent of the school, from the age of twenty-three to thirty. An example of Zeng's style of teaching is recorded in Lu's *Jottings from an Old Scholar's Cottage (Lao-xue-an bi-ji).*[10]

Mr. Tea Mountain said, "Xu Shi-chuan [so far unidentified] imitated Jing Gong [Wang An-shi (1021–86]'s 'Carefully counting fallen petals, because of sitting a long time,/Slowly seeking fragrant grasses, thus returned late' by writing 'Tiny fallen plum blossoms, how to count them? /Leisured walking (amid) fragrant grasses, footsteps thus slowed.' "

At first I did not understand his meaning, but after some time I got it. No doubt Shi-chuan modelled his work exclusively on Tao Yuan-ming. Tao Yuan-ming's poetry always expresses his meaning quite freely and it does not reside in the natural objects [i.e., the meaning does not reside in the natural objects themselves]. For example, "I catch sight of the distant southern hills," (*you-ran jian nan-shan*); that is how Su Dong-po (1037–1101) knew that he definitely was not gazing from afar at the southern hills [i.e., the southern hills were a symbol of some deeper meaning, as Hightower has shown so well]. Today when one [meaning Wang An-shi] writes "Carefully counting fallen petals" and "Slowly seeking fragrant grasses," his meaning *is* deeply embedded in the things themselves, [i.e., he really is doing those things mentioned]. Jing Gong often used Yuan-ming's words with the meaning changed. For example, "Although there's a wattle gate, often want it closed;/The clouds

are still aimless, can rise from the peaks," [lines changed slightly
from Tao's "Return," lines twenty-six and twenty-nine.] When he
wanted to use a character, he could do so; but none of them follow
Yuan-ming's original meaning.

Such was the Jiangxi style of literary criticism: primarily dis-
cussions of how some contemporary poet used the lines or
phrases from some famous poet of the past, especially from
poets of the High Tang period. They called this sort of imitation
"collecting lines" (ji-ju) or "transforming the bones" (huan-gu).
Lu learned this style of literary criticism as well as the correct
methods of verbal parallelism and tonal antithesis required by
Regulated Verse (lü-shi) poetry and other "Mysterious Secrets"
from Zeng Ji; but, most importantly, he was led by Zeng toward
the reading and study of the poets of the Tang dynasty, especially
Li Bo and Du Fu.

In keeping with the special relationship existing in traditional
Chinese society between students and teachers, Lu always respected Zeng Ji both as a man and a teacher. In all of his writings
he has nothing but the highest praise for Zeng, although he never
really says anything specific about the nature of Zeng's verse.[11]
He completely rejected, however, the Jiangxi School conception
that excellence in poetry consists in technical virtuosity. Four
lines from a poem, "Answer to Zheng Yu-ren," present a good
example of this attitude. It was written at age fifty-eight.[12]

> Literary works really should scale the heights of Qu and Song:
> Million mile blue empyrean sending down twin phoenixes!
> "Dainty, delicate, round, and beautiful"—that's not
>     beyond compare.
> Critical claims about "pure marbles" have only deluded men!

Lü Ju-ren once quoted with great approval Xie Tiao's (464–99)
assertion that "fine poetry flows and turns, round and beautiful
like a marble" (hao shi liu-zhuan, yuan-mei ru dan-wan). The
term yuan-mei refers primarily to excellence of form. By praising
Qu Yuan and Song Yu (3rd Cent. B.C.) of the Li Sao and Chu
Elegies tradition, Lu is again calling for poetry that is individualistic, lyrical, and on a grand scale thematically. In his view, fine
poetry does not have to be yuan-mei, formally perfect, but it

should be *hao-fang*, "heroic and unrestrained"; at least that was his view throughout his middle period. "Twin phoenixes" (*luan-feng*), representing both Qu Yuan and Song Yu, are mythical birds often mentioned in the Chu poems, which, by loose analogy, are sometimes compared to the phoenix of the European tradition. In Chu symbolism they represent heroic men as opposed to small men, but fine poets as opposed to mere imitative poetasters in the present context.

## II  *The* Book of Songs:
### *Poetry As Social Criticism and Moral Education*

In keeping with traditional educational practice among the scholar elite, Lu You read and memorized the *Book of Songs* (*Shi Jing*) from about the age of ten. Ever since Confucius was reported to have advised his son to study the *Songs* as a guide to proper moral and political conduct, this anthology of folk songs, court hymns, laments, and eulogies of the Zhou period had been an essential tool of Chinese education. Heavily freighted with moral and allegorical explications, all young men were required to commit the interpretations to memory along with the songs themselves. This style of interpretation, combined with the dubious tradition that the songs were originally collected by the court in order to learn the complaints of the people, gave rise to the belief that the primary purpose of poetry was didactic: to criticise and remonstrate with the rulers and to transform the people through education (*jiao-hua*).

Lu most uncritically believed in this tradition. References to the *Songs* abound in his collection, most of them in poems of doubtful merit, and there can be no doubt that he read and cherished the *Songs* throughout his life.[13] The main influence of the *Songs* on his poetry was his belief that poetry should embody serious social concern. His poems in the heroic-patriotic mode are replete with allusions to the *Songs,* as are the many poems he wrote criticising the treatment of the peasants and the poor by the ruling elite and landed gentry. His poems written specifically about the *Songs,* however, are didactic, traditionalistic, pedantic, and unoriginal—just the sort of thing one would expect a Confucian father to write for his sons' edification.

Lu was most fond of the "Seventh Month" (*qi-yue*) song and the "Airs of Bin" (*bin-feng*) and he often alluded to them in his own poetry. "Reading the Airs of Bin" was written at the age of eighty-two. This seven character poem in the Regulated Verse genre laments the passing of the *Songs* tradition of using poetry (and music) to educate the people in the "Pure Customs" (*chunfeng*) of the ancients.[14]

> In Bin Air's "Seventh Month" song I read
> Works of Sages and Worthies in every stanza.
> Not just because the Kingly Patrimony flourished then;
> 4    More importantly, Pure Customs had not yet vanished.
> Lingering notes of Qu and Song long since gone,
> Who's to transmit the older music of Yao and Shun?
> What my generation learned was not mere "punctuation."
> 8    White haired, by blue lamplight, tears flow freely.

The "Kingly Patrimony" (*wang-ye*) refers to the tradition of the sage kings Yao and Shun that was passed on to the Zhou kings and still flourished, so the Confucianists believed, at the time when the "Seventh Month" song was performed at the Zhou court. Lu not only lamented the decline of the *Songs* tradition but also regretted that the *Li Sao* tradition of fearless criticism of the powers that be (represented again by Qu Yuan and Song Yu) had also fallen into deep decline by his day. He says that students at that time study only the "punctuation" (*zhang-ju*) of the classics, the putting together of readable editions with commentaries, and thus have only a superficial grasp of the letter of the classics but no understanding of their real meaning and significance.

### III   *Qu Yuan and Poetry as the Lyrical Expression of Sentiments*

At the very beginning of his middle period, at the age of forty-five, one stage of his arduous journey from Hangzhou to Kui-zhou in Sichuan took him through Jing-zhou and Jiang-ling (in modern Hubei Province) near the site of Ying, the ancient capital of the Chu state. We may be certain that Lu would have read the *Chu Elegies* and especially Qu Yuan's *Li Sao* during the seven years of his poetic apprenticeship under Zeng Ji, but as a young man with little experience they probably did not make much of an impression on him then. As he passed through Ying, however, now older and wiser and himself an exile from the capital where the emperor had refused to listen to his advice, he began to ponder deeply the lessons of Qu Yuan's life and poetry. Like many Chinese poets who found themselves in similar circumstances, he immediately identified his own situation with that of the semihistorical Qu Yuan and began to write poetry overflowing with lyrical self-dramatization and passionate lament. Later on he would borrow much of the vocabulary of the *Sao* poet and Li Bo to write imaginative poetry full of drunken hyperbole, but the first lesson he learned from Qu Yuan was to express his melancholy sentiments regarding the passing of time, his own sense of personal failure, and the sad state of national affairs.

"Lament for Ying" (*ai-ying*) is the title of two seven character regulated poems written in Jing-zhou near Ying.[15] The title itself is that of one of the "Nine Declarations" (*jiu-zhang*) from the *Chu Elegies*. Lu believed, although modern scholarship no longer accepts the attribution, that the original poem was written by Qu Yuan. Employing an "almost pathological introspectiveness," it details the grief and sorrow of a loyal official who has been exiled to a far country. The first line of the original poem might well have been read by Lu as applying to his own situation exactly, "High Heaven [read the emperor] is not constant in its dispensations: /See how the country is moved to unrest and error!"[16] Lu's lament is, of course, for Hangzhou.

> Linking ancient Shang and Zhou, a reign most long;
> Allying northern Qi and Jin, a mighty power struggle.
> Flower Terrace song and dance finally still and silent;
> 4  Cloud Dream wind and mist yet a green-blue haze.
> Weeds choke ancient palaces where geese nest;
> Bandits cross desolate graves where foxes hide.
> *Li Sao* did not exhaust Qu Yuan's regret:
> 8  Valiant knights, a thousand autumns, tears flow down!

His family originally came from the area of Chu, and Lu saw the Chu state as the rightful heir to the reigns of the great

Shang and Zhou dynasties of Chinese antiquity. Allying itself
with the states of Qi and Jin to its north, Chu struggled with
the state of Qin for control of all China during the Warring
States period. Unfortunately, Lu believed, due to the failure
of the Chu kings to follow the advice of Qu Yuan (just as
Emperor Xiao-zong had failed to follow Lu's advice) and their
insistence on following instead a course of appeasement toward
Qin (just as the Sung appeased the Jürched Jin state), the
Qin state defeated Chu and established the first Chinese Empire.

The "Flower Terrace" was built by King Ling of Chu, and
"Cloud Dream" was the name of a marsh or lake (*yun-meng ze*
or *hu*) in Hubei near the Ying site, as well as having sexual
overtones as a night of romance. The "song and dance" and the
romantic life of the kings of Chu passed into oblivion due to
their ignorance of polity and the relentless passage of time.
Lines three to six are faithful to the tone of the original poem,
line twenty of which reads, "In my exile I did not know that
the palace was now a mound [my "graves"]; /And who would
have thought that East Gate would become a wilderness?"[17]
The warning for the Sung is obvious. Lu perpetuates Qu Yuan's
regret, since he is one of the "valiant knights" (*zhi-shi*) whose
tears flow for the fate of the nation.

The second poem is more personal, more a lament for himself
than for Ying or Hangzhou.

> Jing-zhou, tenth month, early plum spring;
> Past years really riding down hill wheels.
> Why do Heaven and Earth impoverish brave warriors?
> 4  From of old rivers and lakes have harbored
>        suppressed ministers.
> Soaked and sodden, deeply drinking, high pavilion, dusk.
> Sorrow stricken, sadly singing, white hairs increase.
> Want to mourn for Flower Terrace; no place to look:
> 8  Ruined wall, frost and dew dampen thistles and thorns.

Lu sees himself as the "brave warrior" (*zhuang-shi*) and the
"suppressed minister" (*ji-chen*) who has been rejected by his
prince, like Qu Yuan of old, and forced to travel the "rivers
and lakes" (*jiang-hu*), traditional abode of outcast officials, world
rejecting hermits, and bandit heroes of all kinds. He continued

to read and enjoy the *Li Sao,* usually when drinking, for the rest of his life, and his collection is replete with references to it, which are generally paired with ones to the *Book of Changes.*[18] After Qu Yuan, however, Lu discovered an alter ego much closer to his own time.

## IV   *Du Fu and the Building of a Poetic Self-Image*

Of course Lu did not discover Du Fu's poetry in Sichuan; he had read and studied it with Zeng Ji at Shang-rao. In Kui-zhou in 1170, however, he discovered Du Fu the man. He found in Du Fu a perfect self-image: a man of truly heroic stature and talent who was forced by circumstances beyond his control to live in poverty and exile, forever incapable of fulfilling his great dreams. Lu's *Descriptive Record of Du Fu's Lofty Studio at East Encampment,* written at Kui-zhou at the age of forty-five, gives a poignant delineation of that self-image.[19] After relating that Du Fu seemed to have had at least three Lofty Studio (*gao-zhai*) dwellings around Kui-zhou, but that all of them had fallen into ruin and were gone without a trace, Lu comments that only East Encampment (*dong-tun*), owned by a man named Li Xiang, who asked him to write this description, still survived. He continues:

...I heave a great sigh and say: Du Fu was an officer of the world. Early on he met Ming Huang (the Bright Emperor) and (his son) Su-zong. Although the offices held were not outstandingly respected, their appreciation of him was truly deep so that he once confidently compared himself to Sage Emperor Shun's great officers Ji and Qi.

Then when he was dispirited and downcast in Sichuan, he was moved by the history of Liu Bei's Prime Minister Zhu-ge Liang and often wrote of him in his poetry, in rhythms that are sad and strong and repeatedly moving. His scope and purpose were indeed great! He was away from the capital longer and longer, however, and the various officials knew well of his poverty; but not one of them lifted a finger to help him. When he reached Kui-zhou and served under Bo Mao-lin and Yan Wu, he was like a nine foot stalwart (*zhang-fu*) bending his back to squeeze in under a low roof; if he wanted to spit out a breath, there was no way!

When I read his poems and come to the lines, "Late in life I

offer a last fellowship to young men,/ Who show affection to my
face and laugh behind my back," I cannot keep my tears from flowing. Good God! That words could be so sad! The song of Jing Ke
and the weeping of Ruan Ji (210–63) could not surpass them.

Du Fu did not only narrowly and pettily apply himself to official
advancement. His love for his prince and his anxiety for his country
were without compare. He wanted to employ what he had learned
from study to aid the Son of Heaven to reestablish the order of the
great Tang ages of *zhen-guan* and *kai-yuan* [627–50 and 713–42, the
prosperous parts of the reigns of Tai-zong and Ming Huang], but the
older he got the more absurd became his destiny, until he died a
failure. Thus he is not deserving of our blame for such sadness in
his verse.

Today Master Li has chosen from the beginning not to tread the
path of glory and ignominy seeking office. He reads, plays the lute,
and sings; suddenly forgetting that he is old. Not having Du Fu's
worries, he has his loftiness and ease. Du Fu lived at East Encampment for only one year, but Master Li's family has lived here
for several generations. If the dead could return to life, I really do
not know whether Du Fu would say that he or Master Li enjoyed the
best of the situation.

As for me, in office I cannot but stand ashamed before my duty;
but if I retire I have no land to cultivate. Thus I truly envy Master
Li, and so was happy to have written this record. [dated 4/10/1171]

From the age of forty-five until his death at eighty-four,
hardly a year went by that Lu did not write at least one poem
in which he mentioned Du Fu. He praised Du Fu's poetry in
broad and glowing terms, expressed his admiration for his patriotism and genius, and lamented his poverty and the fact that
his policies and governmental talents went unused. In all of
these things, Lu was quite consciously referring to himself. He
also used lines from Du Fu's poems in many of his own works,
but generally not in his most characteristic and best poems.
He never really imitated or parodied Du Fu's style; at least
no poems of this kind have survived. The real influence of his
reading of Du Fu was in the formation of his self-image, especially during his passionately patriotic middle period, and in
the overall tone of his poetry. Du Fu, like the *Songs* that he
himself followed, taught Lu to write strong and vigorous poetry
full of passionate lyricism and abiding social concern, to write

poetry that was at once beautiful in form and grand in scope.[20]

Du Fu left Changan out of disappointment at his failure to achieve a significant public career in the summer of 759. He travelled westward to Qin-zhou in modern Gansu, then south from there to Tong-gu, and later to Chengdu in Sichuan, where he arrived in the twelfth month. He lived in his celebrated Thatched Hut in Chengdu for nearly three years, enjoying to the full the quiet and well-being of his later years. He was forced by a local revolt to leave Chengdu and wander around Sichuan from the sixth month of 762 until the spring of 764, when he returned to Chengdu to serve as military advisor to the Prefect Yan Wu. In the first month of 765 he gave up this office, and in the spring of 766 moved to Kui-zhou, where he lived until the spring of 768; it was during this time that he wrote many of his last and best poems. The final three years of his life, from 768 to the winter of 770, he spent "appropriately enough, since wandering had steadily become the grand theme of that life, in travels within the area which forms the modern provinces of Hubei and Hunan."[21] He died in the late autumn or winter of 770 while once more thinking of returning to Changan.

Lu had all of these things in mind, as well as their relation to himself, in the summer of 1171 when he wrote the seven character Regulated Verse poem "Climbing White Emperor City Tower At Night and Thinking of Du Fu" in Kui-zhou.[22]

> White-haired Du Fu, who pitied him,
> Alone, sadly chanting poems throughout Sichuan?
> Men built flying towers . . . all gone today.
> 4  Waves churn lone moon . . . just as before.
> Rising and sinking for all time, an infinite process.
> Ignorant and wise alike succumb, finite their years.
> This theme, cold, sad, who's to share it?
> 8  Night deepens, gulls and egrets fly up from the sand.

"Succumb" is literally "return" (*gui*) and means, of course, to die. Line five very nicely carries on the water image of line four, contrasting the eternal "rising and sinking" (*sheng-chen*) of the waves, the same waves that Du Fu saw as symbolic of man's limited span of years, thus voicing the sadly lyrical manner

typical of Tang poetry. The fine parallelism and antithesis of
these two lines are comparable to lines three and four of Du Fu's
poem, "Climbing the Yue-yang Tower," which we know Lu was
very fond of. Line eight may also be compared to lines seven
and eight of Du Fu's poem, "Expressing My Thoughts While
Traveling At Night": "Drifting drifting, what [am I] like? / A
solitary sandgull (*sha-ou*) between Heaven and Earth." Lu may
well have wished that Du's spirit inhabited one of the "gulls"
(*ou*) that flew up from the "sand" (*sha*) to share his sadness
with him, sadness at the rapid passage of time and the fates of
both Du Fu and himself, both of whom were forced to wander
far from their beloved capitals.[23]

In his late sixties, when he was giving more and more thought
to literary criticism and poetic style, Lu strongly defended Du
Fu's poetry against his imitators in the following untitled essay.[24]

When people today criticise Du Fu's poetry, they only seek out
the origins of his diction and do not understand his meaning (*yi*).
Criticism should not be done this way in the first place. For example
Du's "Yue-yang Tower" poem, "Long ago heard of Dong-ting's waters,/ Today mount Yue-yang Tower./ Wu and Chu cleaved east and
south,/ Heaven and Earth float day and night./ Of family and friends,
not one word;/ Old and sick, with a solitary boat./ A warhorse north
of the passes,/ Lean on railing, tears gush and flow." How can one
look for the origins of his diction in this? Even if you could find
origins for each and every word, you would just be farther away
from Du Fu's meaning.

No doubt later people simply do not understand wherein Du Fu's
poetry is amazingly superior to ancient and contemporary verse; they
only consider the fact that a particular phrase has an origin [i.e.,
has been used in someone else's earlier poetry] as true skill. For
example the poems in the *Xi-kun chou-chang-ji*: there is not one
word that does not have its origin, and they think that *they* follow
and equal Du Fu. What nonsense! Moreover when my contemporaries compose poems, their words just might not be without origins.
Perhaps they do not even know it themselves. Then someone writes
a commentary and finds that every word has its origin, but it still
does not prevent them from being terribly bad poems!

This essay, with its criticism of a particularly Chinese "scholarly"
type of phrase matching, with no attempt to establish true influ-

ence, still has a certain relevance, and it is probably the most complete repudiation of the Jiangxi style to be found among Lu's collected works.

The following five character regulated poem, "Reading Li's and Du's Poems," written at eighty-one, offers Lu's final judgment of the poetry of Du Fu and Li Bo, as well as expressing his confidence that his own poetry will insure his fame long after his death. These great works of art will live on "eternally new (or renewed) like Nature in its flower" (*chang yu wu-hua xin*).[25]

> Brocade Wash boundless blue wanderer.
> Green Lotus wave wandering bard.
> Talent and fame filling Heaven and Earth;
> 4 Life's fate aging in wind and dust.
> Most difficult for scholars to find patrons;
> Which of us is not lowly and poor?
> Their books remain by my bright window,
> 8 Eternally new like Nature in its flower!

Du Fu called himself the "wanderer of the boundless blue" (*cang-lang-ke*) when he lived by the Flower Washing Stream, also known as "Brocade Wash" (*zhuo-jin*), in Chengdu. Li Bo called himself the "wave wandering one" (*dan-dang-ren*) as well as the "Recluse of Green Lotus" (*qing-lian ju-shi*).[26] Legend has it that Li Bo drowned while returning from exile in the south of China, and that Du Fu died of hunger while still in Sichuan. Whatever the truth of these stories, Lu believed that both poets ended their days "lowly and poor" (*jian-pin*) just as he felt himself to be at the time.

If Du Fu's life and poetry influenced the public side of Lu's personality, the example of Li Bo appealed to him in personal terms and reinforced his own flamboyant tendencies.

## V  *Li Bo and Reckless Romanticism*

From the time that he entered Chengdu "riding a donkey through Sword Gate in a fine rain," as Li Bo had ridden before, Lu's personality became increasingly eccentric, as we have seen, and he began to write highly imaginative poetry that Chinese

critics like to call *lang-man,* sometimes translated "romantic," by
which they usually mean individualistic and imaginative. This
was the time when "strange, wondrous images jutted out/ like
rocks washed by thunderous torrents"; and for many years after
that Lu wrote many drinking and dream poems very similar in
style to those of Li Bo. We will examine them at length in two
later chapters. Here I would like to quote just one seven
character Ancient Verse poem entitled "Brocade Pavilion" that
seems to capture a mood very much like that of Li Bo's poems
and lifestyle. It was written late in 1175 and describes a party
with the poet Fan Cheng-da (1126–93) in Chengdu.[27]

> Heavenly Duke, thinking of my mouth and tongue,
> Bestows delicious golden oranges and red lichees.
> Pitying as well my crazy eyes, older yet crazier,
> 4 Let's me see Guang-ling peonies, Sichuan begonias.
> Travelling widely ten thousand *li* following my pleasure,
> Heavenly Duke has really not treated me too badly.
> You great ones cannot leave Changan City;
> 8 Fettered indeed by jewelled belt and flowered sash.
> What pleasure today to follow Master Stone Lake!
> His great generosity overlooks Deaf Cheng's deafness!
> Nightly revelling in new pavilion under crab apple trees,
> 12 Pouring and sipping crimson clouds from clear crystal cups.
> Lute strings gaily strumming, waist drums quicken;
> Swirling phoenix dancing skirts, moist musky mist!
> Spring wine, cups overflowing, candle glow shimmers;
> 16 White moon, sky centered, flowers' shadows stand.
> Guests like clouds circle our jade pavilion;
> Poems not yet on paper, already traded and sung!
> Rhymes and rhythms of this locale today made new:
> 20 Noble scions of Phoenix Pavilion here's your true model!

In the first eight lines Lu rather ironically contrasts his experiences in travelling thousands of miles from home with those of
the "great ones" (*gui-ren,* "noble people") at court who never
leave the comforts of the capital, with Changan signifying
Hangzhou. He has indeed grown in experience and in poetic
power since leaving home. All in all, he writes, the "Heavenly
Duke" (*tian-gong*), Emperor Xiao-zong, has really been good
to him in banishing him to far off Sichuan. His celebrated rela-

tionship with Fan Cheng-da is eloquent testimony that he was not fettered by "jeweled belt" (*bao-dai*) and "flowered sash" (*hua-ying*, really a hat string), conventional symbols of official rank.

The rest of the poem, then, describes their unfettered life in Chengdu. "Stone Lake" (*shi-hu*) was Fan's favorite nickname. Line nine is an allusion to a story about Huang Ba of the Han dynasty who generously kept in his employ an old and deaf official named Xu Cheng against the recommendations of others because, "although he is old he can still bow to receive and send off guests."[28] Lines thirteen and fourteen describe the dancing girls twisting and turning in their phoenix-patterned skirts until the perspiration mingles with their perfume to create an overpowering fragrance. This is the sort of spectacle and imagery that Li Bo revelled in.

Lines fifteen and sixteen seem very close to Li Bo's famous poem, "Drinking Alone Under the Moon," (*yue-xia du-zhuo*) lines one to four: "A pot of wine among the flowers, / Drinking alone with no one near. / Raising the cup, invite the bright moon, / With my shadow making three men." And in line nine of Li's poem, the image "When I sing the moon goes to and fro . . ." *in the wine cup* is echoed in Lu's poem, where the candle light shimmers in the wine as it overflows the cups, and the flowers' shadows stand erect in the moon's bright reflection.

Lines nineteen and twenty proudly complete the poem by boasting of the effect that the poetry of Fan and Lu is having on the verse of their day. Lu admonishes the "noble scions of Phoenix Pavilion" (*feng-ge she-ren*), the "great ones" of line seven above, to follow their model both in poetry and lifestyle. *Feng-ge she-ren*, incidentally, is a good example of the use of contemporary colloquial language in Lu's poetry. Originally a Tang dynasty nickname for court officials, it came to mean "young nobles" (*gong-zi*) in general in the Sung, hence my "noble scions."

## VI  *Cen Shen and Border Style Patriotism*

While in Sichuan, Lu served for a time in Shu-zhou not far from Chengdu, and there he read and edited the poetry of the well-known Tang dynasty "border style" poet Cen Shen. Cen's poetry directly influenced the style and diction of Lu's heroic-patriotic poetry. These works will be discussed later, but here I would like to offer one seven character Ancient Verse poem entitled "Drunken Song" as an example of a poem written in a style similar to Cen's verse.[29]

> Times past one drunk I'd down barrels and buckets,
> While others there drinking water couldn't keep pace.
> Crossing lances, striking swords, hardly seemed heroic;
> 4 Brandishing brush right and left, wind and rain arose!
> Meeting in the snow, hunting beneath South Mountain,
> Clear dawn lofty peaks, a thousand feet of jade.
> Roadside foxes and hares not worth our pursuit;
> 8 Crossing over West Village seeking tiger tracks.
> Sable robe half removed, horse like a dragon,
> Raising whip, pointing standard, breath spitting rainbows!
> No need holding bows, guarding our near frontiers;
> 12 Pass the command, clean away the Hunnish stench!
> Little Huns, hiding and killing for sixty years,
> Yap, yap like mad dogs whose strength is spent.
> Our holy court, rather than kill your cubs,
> 16 Will return you to your old den east of Liao.

The poem recalls his life on the border at Nan-zheng, riding and hunting, and concludes with the usual call for an attack on the Jürched state of Jin in the north. "Breath" ($qi$) in line ten may also be translated as "spirit," "elan," "energy," "vitality," and so on. It is the one quality that Lu believed during his middle period to be most important in both poetry and personality. He repeatedly refers to "breath spitting rainbows" ($qi\ tu\ hong$), an hyperbolic description of the preternatural powers of a knight errant ($you$-$xia$) or hero ($hao$-$xia$), to describe his own feelings of exuberance and superiority to the effete and, as he saw them, cowardly courtiers of his time. The Jürched "Huns" as dogs is a poetic turn on a very old Chinese way of viewing the various nomadic peoples that inhabited their borders.[30]

### VII  *Tao Yuan-ming and Quiet Resistance in Adversity*

Lu read Tao Yuan-ming's poetry before that of any other poet, and he was profoundly influenced by the example of Tao's life and verse, the primary message of which may be summed up as "quiet resistance in adversity." After he retired, at sixty-four, Lu began to write pastoral and philosophical poems expressing a philosophy increasingly like that of Tao Yuan-ming. From then on hardly a year went by that he did not write at least one poem mentioning Tao, and there are more references to Tao in his collection than to any other single poet, matched only by references and allusions to the *Zhuang Zi*.[31] Unlike his Du Fu references, allusions to Tao usually occur in very fine poems, or at least in poems that are typical of Lu's mature style.

His reading of Tao helped him to resist the adversity of old age and to transcend the problems of this world, problems that had so occupied his mind during his middle period. "Letting the Brush Write Under the Pines No. 3" is a fine example of a seven character quatrain written early in his third period at the age of sixty-six.[32]

> Jade-growing mushroom-eating arts untransmitted;
> Trying a hand at Alchemy is even more uncertain.
> I once received Master Tao's marvelous secret:
> Just listen to pine winds—spontaneously reach
> transcendence!

"Jade-growing" (*zhong-yu*) is an allusion to the story of Yang Bo, who was given a bushel of stones by an adept; he planted them and they grew into jade pieces.[33] "Mushroom-eating" (*can-zhi*) refers to the ingestion of magic mushrooms in order to achieve physical immortality. It is probable that Lu had begun his alchemical experiments by this time and was rather dissatisfied with the results. He remained skeptical of the use of such outside aids to longevity. Far better simply to sit down under the pine trees, symbolic of longevity and resistance themselves, and hold "unconscious intercourse with beauty old as creation" (Wordsworth), and in that manner become an immortal transcendent (*xian*) spontaneously from within.

"Reading Tao's Poetry" is a five character regulated poem in which Lu admits that he has tried to follow Tao's poetic style and failed, but that he has had better luck in copying Tao's eccentric and quietist lifestyle.[34]

> My poems envy Tao Yuan-ming's,
> Regret not recreating his subtlety.
> Resigning, returning, also too late;
> 4    In drinking wine, perhaps nearly equal.
> Light rain, hoeing melon patch;
> Moonlight, sitting on fishing rock.
> A thousand years and no such man;
> 8    With whom shall I go home!

Tao retired early from office rather than be caught up in the political strife of his time, retaining both his pride and his integrity, not to mention his life. In retirement he lived the life of a gentleman farmer, poet, and philosopher. Since Lu's own retirement had come much later in life, after serving in many minor and insignificant offices, thus exhausting his patience and his strength, he envied Tao's spirit of detachment and freedom. His poetry may not be as good as Tao's, he writes modestly, but his lifestyle—drinking, gardening, and fishing—can be. Tao often did all of these things, and there was even a rock at Chai-sang near Jiu-jiang on which he was said to have slept when he was drunk; the eighteenth century poet Yuan Mei once visited the place and wrote a poem about it.[35]

"Walking to Pu-kou Before It Rained" is a five character Ancient Verse poem, written in his eighty-first year, that expresses very clearly Lu's resolve to resist adversity in conscious emulation of Tao Yuan-ming.[36]

> Rain falls, thousand hills darken;
> Wind rises, myriad trees howl.
> Liberated mind forgets world's affairs,
> 4    Leisured steps leave marshy arbor.
> Rustic spot knows only withdrawal,
> Heart's expectations never again heroic.
> Song Qing distributes fine medicines;
> 8    Xu Gu offers his new silk robe.
> Rather beg for old Tao's food;
> Hard to sup Qu Yuan's dregs.
> Concentrate the mind to exhaust *Changes* and *Lao*,
> 12    With remaining strength study *Zhuang* and *Sao*.
> Cane and clogs often walking for pleasure,
> Hoe and rake accustomed to working hard.

Should I die this morning or evening,
16 I've stilll sufficiently reached my high!

The first six lines set the scene of Lu's seclusion and then two allusions depict the generous manner in which the local people treat him in his retirement. Song Qing sold medicine to the wealthy officials at West Market in Changan during the Tang dynasty, but he always sold at a discount or even gave away medicines to impoverished scholars. Xu Gu of the Warring States period helped his poor retainer Fan Zhui to make a start on the road to fame. Later when Fan had become a prime minister at the Qin court, he returned dressed in rags to test Xu's friendship, and Xu immediately gave him the silk robe he was wearing. Fan was so moved that he left his high post and returned to serve under Xu once more.

Tao Yuan-ming was often in very bad straits during his retirement and once had to beg for food due to crop failures, but he thus survived in adversity and continued to write his philosophical verse. Qu Yuan, on the other hand, allowed his self-pity to overpower him and committed suicide by drowning in the Mi-lo River. Lu preferred Tao's course of philosophical resistance to Qu's useless self-destruction. The rest of this poem describes how he lived as Tao did, studying the *Lao Zi*, the *Zhuang Zi*, the *Book of Changes*, and the *Li Sao*, walking in the countryside, working in the fields—enjoying "life's everyday experiences ... whence spiritual dignity originates" (Wordsworth), experiences "sufficient to reach my high (transcendence)" (*zu sui wu gao*).

Line ten comes from "The Fisherman" (*yu-fu*) poem in the *Chu Elegies*, a Daoist style anecdote about a simple fisherman who scolds the exiled Qu Yuan for his arrogance and self-martyrdom and urges him to seek official employment when times are good and to retire when times are bad, just what Tao Yuan-ming in fact did. Lines ten and eleven of that poem are, "If all the world is muddy, why not help them to stir up the mud and beat up the waves? / And if all men are drunk, why not sup (*bu*) their dregs (*zao*) and swill their lees?"[37] Lu's love of wine never abated in old age, and he endorses these sentiments wholeheartedly.

Confucius once said, "In the morning hear the Way; in the

evening, die content!" (*zhao wen dao, xi si ke yi*).[38] Like Jung's
archetype of the "old man who has seen enough" and like
Confucius himself, Lu had achieved his feeling of transcendence,
for the moment at least, after a life of struggle and spiritual
quest.

As the years went by, Lu's admiration for Tao's poetry grew,
and he became especially interested in the pastoral aspects of
it. At the same time that he was establishing his own deepest
communion with nature, he praised Tao's poetry along with that
of Xie Ling-yun (385–433), who is usually mentioned together
with Tao as a great landscape poet. "Reading Tao's Poems," a
seven character quatrain written at the age of eighty-three,
sums up his praise of these two poets and refers particularly to
Tao's poem, "On Reading the Classic of the Hills and Seas"
(*du shan-hai jing*).[39]

> Tao and Xie's literary works equal the Creation;
> Poems perfected could make ghosts and spirits grieve.
> Just read the line, "summer trees grow green";
> Would you require a poet to say anything more!

## VIII   Mei Yao-chen and Poems Calm as Water

Early in 1203, when Lu was seventy-eight, a relative of the
Northern Sung poet Mei Yao-chen asked him to write a preface
to a collection of Mei's poetry. Lu had read Mei's verse for
many years and had even written many poems in imitation of
Mei's style, but prior to this time Mei seems to have had very
little influence on Lu's much more vigorous style. The way in
which his imitative poems follow Mei is that they are nearly all
five character Ancient Verse poems concerning very ordinary
subjects, such as oranges, mosquitos, inkstones, and ghosts and
marvels. At seventy-eight, however, when he was well into his
own quiet period, Lu was quite captivated by these poems by
Mei and praised them very highly in his preface. He regarded
Mei as the best poet of the early Northern Sung period prior
to Su Dong-po, his poetry being equal to the prose of the great
Ou-yang Xiu (1007–1072), who was also the initiator of the new
style in Sung poetry that Mei and Su perfected. Lu singled out

Mei's diction for special praise, hyperbolic praise that is singularly unedifying in that he does not really tell us anything concrete about Mei's use of words.[40]

"Reading Mei Yao-chen's Poems," a five character Regulated Verse poem written at age seventy-nine, praises Mei's naturalness and ease of composition using Daoist images primarily from the *Zhuang Zi*. In praising Mei, Lu is also commenting on his own late style.[41]

> Li and Du no longer write;
> Master Mei is truly great!
> Not merely "transforming old bones,"
> 4 But opening up "doors of perception."
> Unstinting work, his training-discipline;
> Deeply flowing, his origin-springs.
> A lifetime of ox-cutting skill
> 8 Left "plenty of room" for cuts and turns.

Lu first praises Mei as the best poet since Li Bo and Du Fu. In an earlier period, he had offered the same high praise for Cen Shen, but his critical standards as well as his personality had changed greatly since then. "Transforming old bones" (*gu-huan*) originally referred to the Daoist belief that meditation could lead to a transformation of one's earthly body into an immortal "astral body." As mentioned above, the term was also used by the Jiangxi School critics to refer to the correct way to imitate the Tang poets. "Opening up doors of perception" (Blake's term) (*ding-men kai*) refers to the Buddhist and Daoist belief that during very deep meditation the top of the head (*ding-men*) literally opens up (*kai*); this opening is equivalent to enlightenment or the achievement of a new way of perception. With these two images Lu is saying that Mei Yao-chen not only learned from the poets of the past, but also equalled and even surpassed them, opening up many new areas of awareness in Chinese poetry. Mei's primary contribution to Chinese poetry was, in fact, the broadening of the scope and content of the *shi* (lyric) style, extending it especially into the realms of simple and commonplace events and objects.[42]

The last four lines describe Mei's technical mastery of the

creative art, the "ease" or "calmness" (*ping-dan*) born of "discipline and training" (*duan-lian*) that characterized his mature style. Mei wrote that his poetry was "composed with great effort and care ... striving to follow the *Da-ya* and *Xiao-ya* sections of the *Book of Songs*."[43] The final couplet offers once again Lu's favorite allusion to the artless art of perfect concentration that was the essence of creativity for him as well as the method of "nurturing life" (*yang-sheng*)—the story of Cook Ding from chapter three of the *Zhuang Zi*. Cook Ding cut up oxen for nineteen years without ever once sharpening his blade because he did not perceive the ox with his eyes but with his "spirit" (*shen*) and he followed the "natural makeup" (*tian-li*), moving the knife with the "greatest subtlety" (*shen-wei*); thus he had "plenty of room—more than enough for the blade to play about" (*hui-hui hu, qi yu you ren bi you yu-di yi*).[44] In his later period, Lu believed that his own technical mastery and his very perception of the world around him was altered, and he projected this belief onto the earlier poet.

In "Autumn Thoughts No. 4," written at age seventy-nine, Lu described his own late verse in terms similar to those generally applied to Mei Yao-chen.[45]

> Poems calm like water, Art slightly improves.
> Body lonely like a cloud, cares gradually lighten.
> Fallen leaves cover fence, gate, lane, evening.
> One thin rattan cane, short leisured stroll.

Lu's late period poems are "calm like water" (*ru shui dan*) because his "Art" (*gong*), the same *gong* as in *gong-fu*, "skill in the martial arts," which comes from an almost meditative concentration resulting in absolute naturalness of movement, had improved. Cook Ding was, of course, a man who had true creative *gong-fu*. In another poem written at eighty-three Lu wrote, "Little poems, leisured and calm (*xian-dan*) like autumn waters."[46]

## IX  *Late Poems: Transcendence*

In his eighties Lu wrote nothing but Regulated Verse (*lü-shi*) poems, poems written with consummate skill approaching technical perfection and yet freely and spontaneously composed. By that time poetry had become his very way of life, his seclusion from the world of change and impermanence, his escape from time into eternity, his "place of transcendence" (*chao-ran chu*).

"Pleasures of Seclusion," a seven character regulated poem written at age eighty, proudly claims a reclusion deeper than Tao Yuan-ming's, while also describing his late poetry to be spontaneously developing in the direction of "calm and ease" (*ping-dan*) quite "without intention" (*wu-yi*).[47]

> In old age interest in life gradually fades,
> Drifting between water and clouds, I wait on death.
> Tortoise-legged bed's steady on newly cold nights;
> 4   Crane-born letter returns to old hermit's hill.
> Without intention my poems now become flat and calm;
> Ending friendships my dreams too feel pure and leisured.
> In one way I even outdo Tao Yuan-ming:
> 8   My still silent gate isn't even shut!

"Life" is the "floating life" (*fu-sheng*)—vain, fleeting, and insubstantial—that the pitiful world of affairs regards as real. The tortoise and the crane are again used here, this time in a confident and transcendent mood. Like his "tortoise-legged bed" (*gui-chuang*), Lu is resistant and steady on cold winter nights. Like the lofty crane, he is in deep seclusion and will not come out again even if he is summoned by a letter written in "crane calligraphy" (*he-shu*), a particular style of writing said to have been used in ancient times to call hermits out of retirement and into service. Line twenty-six of Tao Yuan-ming's poem "Return" reads: "There is a gate there, but it is always shut."[48] Lu's seclusion is so deep there is no need to shut the gate; no one is going to come and disturb him.

The last poem to be cited here expresses Lu's total satisfaction with his life and poetry. He felt that he had finally achieved the "pure poetry (*qing-shi*) that's repeatedly sung for a thousand ages" that he had hoped for on his way to Sichuan some thirty years earlier.[49] He had achieved it, he felt, in his final period, with his simple yet beautiful poems, written in response to whatever moved him in his everyday life and "achieved with a free and easy brush" (*xin-bi-cheng*). A seven character regu-

lated poem, "Written as the Snow Fell Very Cold," was written
at the age of eighty-three.[50]

> Clouds darken, winds howl, giving me a start.
> An eye blinks and ink pool turns to ice!
> By the window, suddenly lose sparse plum shadows.
> 4 On the pillow, hollowly hear lost goose cry.
> Noble's son in black mink now drinking heartily;
> Peasant family's yellow ox also plowing deeply.
> This old man has a different place of transcendence:
> 8 One pure poem dashed off with free and easy brush!

### CHAPTER 3

# Poetry as an Expression of Patriotism

C HINESE scholars ancient and modern have principally praised Lu You for his heroic and patriotic poetry. The Qing dynasty critic Zhao Yi (1727–1841) used the term "heroic and unrestrained" (*hao-si*) to describe this element in Lu's verse. He even went so far as to state unequivocally that Lu's poetry was superior to that of Su Dong-po, who is much better known to Western readers, precisely because he was more courageous than Su in speaking out in verse against the appeasement policy toward the northern invaders and criticizing the governing elite for the difficult life of the peasant masses.[1] One of the great founders of modern Chinese nationalism, Liang Qi-chao (1873–1929), also praised him as a "patriotic" (*ai-guo*) and "nationalistic" (*min-zu*) poet.[2] High school and college literature courses in Taiwan today still emphasize Lu's patriotic poetry, and modern editors of his collection both in Taiwan and in the People's Republic of China weight their anthologies heavily in favor of his patriotic and socially critical works.

The French scholar Jacques Gernet has painted a picture of the typical upperclass Hangzhou urbanite of the century after Lu died that differs widely from the man Lu You as I have portrayed him in Chapter 1 above.

The upper-class town-dweller of the thirteenth century was a highly-strung person, and even seems, because of his extreme sensitivity to fashion and his love of display and self-dramatization, to have been rather effeminate. Unremitting pursuit of pleasure, over-indulgence in alcohol, and sexual excess drained his energy and accentuated the weaker side of his nature. Often a word or an attitude were, for him, the substitute for an action.[3]

By way of contrast, Lu You was a passionate man of action who worried all his life about the nation and the common people.

In his most active years he actually studied military strategy
and practiced the martial arts of swordsmanship, archery, and
riding. He once killed a tiger singlehandedly with a lance from
horseback. He played polo and hunted until well after his fiftieth
year. His ambition for reconquest of the north frustrated, he did
become eccentric, behaving wildly (*kuang*), drinking heavily,
gambling, and enjoying the company of dancing girls in Chengdu;
but these activities merely helped him through a difficult time
and did not sap his creative energy. Indeed, this extravagant
and romantic period was also the period of his most powerful
and heroic poetry, and it was followed by an even longer period
of prolific poetic output and increasing technical mastery. Lu
was a Confucian scholar by training and tradition, but he was
personally far more interested in Daoism and alchemical in-
vestigations. In his later years he mellowed and accepted himself
more as poet and recluse than military or political genius, but
he never ceased to lament, less passionately perhaps but none-
theless sincerely, the fate of the nation and the failure of his
great ambition.

Throughout his life Lu wrote intensely lyrical and empassioned
poetry, often highly imaginative and original, pouring out his
feelings for his country and his personal conception of the heroic
and patriotic. In this chapter I will discuss several of the best
known and most frequently anthologized of Lu's poems in the
heroic or patriotic mode. The reader should keep in mind from
the outset that for every poem chosen here for translation there
may be as many as a hundred more poems of a similar nature.
I have tried to select the most representative works as well as
those that seemed to me to go well into English translation.

Many of Lu's patriotic poems are forthright appeals for war
and an end to the government's appeasement policy toward the
Jürched. "Feelings on Examining a Map of Da-san Pass," a five
character Ancient Verse poem written in his forty-eighth year
in Sichuan, is a good example.[4]

> Mount horse and attack the crazed barbarians;
> Dismount and dash off military dispatches.
> At twenty I treasured this ambition.

4   At fifty I'm still a scraggy scholar.

Between Da-san and Chen-cang,
Mountain streams wind deep and dark.
Fighting spirit assembles loyal warriors
8  Who share together a brave plan.
Steep and rocky is Xian-yang City,
Ancient capital of Qin and Han.
The royal aura floats on twilight mists;
12  Palaces and halls engender spring weeds.
When can we follow the king's generals,
Sweep the way, receive the royal palanquin?
From Yellow River to Han-gu Pass,
16  Open all roads to boat and cart.
Men and horse depart from Yan and Zhao;
Linen and silk arrive at Qing and Xu.
First we must rebuild the Seven Temples;
20  Next plan out the Nine Royal Roads.
A single division ties up the khan,
Empty the city to view our captives!
Drink "long life!" in Great Peace Palace,
24  Begin a new *Zhen-guan* reign.
If a man fulfilled his desire,
He would not die like an insect.
Ambition greatly overflowing, without appointed time,
28  Drunken courage vainly suffuses my whole being.

The first four lines present the major theme and the *raison d'etre* of the poem—his great "ambition" (*zhi*) to labor in the army, writing military dispatches and fighting the Jürched. Here they are referred to as the "crazed barbarians" (*kuang-hu*); he has even more derogatory epithets for them. Personal and national failure and shame, always in the background of these poems, are also mentioned at the outset as he expresses his frustration at still being a "scraggy scholar" (*qu-ru*) at the age of fifty.

In the next four lines he turns his thoughts to the "land within the passes," Shaanxi, bounded on one side by the Da-san Pass, on the map before him. This land of great historical and strategic significance had given birth to many "loyal warriors" (*yi-shi*) possessed of that heroic "spirit" (*qi*) that urged them on to make "brave plans" (*zhuang-tu*) for establishing powerful Chinese dynasties. The next four lines continue naturally from the "brave plan" of heroes to the goal of their planning—recapture of the "ancient capital of Qin and Han" where the great emperors lived and had their tombs, now so sadly overgrown with "spring weeds" (*chun-wu*). Xian-yang, the Qin capital, stands for Bian-jing (Kaifeng), the capital of the Northern Sung dynasty, as well as for the entire northern territories.

Lines thirteen and fourteen ask the inevitable question: when will we attack and sweep away the Jürched and thus prepare the way for our emperor to return to his rightful capital? Lines fifteen to twenty-four then describe Lu's conception of the reestablishment of Chinese sovereignty over the northern lands. The roads would once again be safe for men and goods. The all-important ceremonial temples would be rebuilt and the proper rites carried out by the Son of Heaven. The khan (*ke-han*), another Han term referring to the Jin ruler, would surrender with his multitudes. The Sung would once again establish an empire to rival the power and glory of the great Tang empire under Tai-zong (Li Shi-min).

After this rapsodic description of revived grandeur, the last four lines return with sadness to the point where the poem began, the actual situation of the poet sitting in his room looking at a map. His "desire" (*yuan*) is still quite unfulfilled, and there seems little prospect of his dream coming to pass. His "ambition" that "overflows like a river in flood" (*da hao*) is completely "without appointed time" (*wu-qi*) and "drunken courage vainly suffuses his whole being" (*zui-dan kong man-qu*).

The diction is typical of Lu's heroic mode. The key words, repeated in poem after poem, are "ambition," "floodlike" here, but more often "brave/strong/heroic" (*zhuang*); "real man/stalwart" (*zhang-fu*); "without appointed time;" "drunken" (*zui*); and "vainly/emptily/to no purpose" (*kong*). Also characteristic are the allusions to the great Han and Tang dynasties as models for the Sung.

Lu's ambition, then, and the goal he urged on his contemporaries in these poems, was always the reestablishment of a glorious and unified Chinese Empire on the Han and Tang dynasty models. As a man of his times, and with absolutely no antimonarchical inclinations, he considered the reestablishment of the emperor and the rites the key element in the reassertion of Chinese cultural values over the entire area traditionally occupied by the Chinese Empire. His patriotism, then, was precisely what the Greek etymology of the word implies: "loyalty to the prince" (*zhong-jun*), loyalty to the Son of Heaven who was in turn the father of his people and the embodiment of the Chinese world order. It also included the other popular Chinese term, *ai-guo,* "love of country," as reverence for Chinese cultural values, the values of the educated elite, as he had absorbed them from the classics since early childhood. Although he criticized his bureaucratic contemporaries, and even the emperor, for not asserting those values forcefully enough, he never attacked the system of monarchy and officialdom upon which the strength of the Chinese nation was seen to be based. He firmly believed that it was precisely this system of ordered government that was most responsible for the great superiority of Chinese culture over all others known to him. His desire, his great ambition, what he had in common with all patriots of every age and clime, was to extend the area of influence of his culture to once again encompass its "rightful" territory and to help his country to rejoin the stream of its "rightful" destiny. Modern Chinese can readily identify with most of his aspirations.

"Feeling Angry," a seven character regulated poem written at the age of fifty-eight, is one of his most famous as well as one of his strongest attacks on the emperor and court officials for their persistence in the appeasement policy.[5]

> Were today's emperor a divine general like Zhou Xuan
> Who would write "South Campaign" or "Northern Expedition"?
> The four seas one family, Heaven made Mandate.
> 4 Two Rivers, hundred states, all Sung lands.
> Court officials still keep appeasement policy;
> Brave warriors vainly waste strong, young years.
> Jing-Lo snow melts, spring returns again;
> 8 Grass grows rank on our Great Emperor's tomb!

The allusions are to the Zhou dynasty and the *Book of Songs.* King Xuan of Zhou (r. 827–782 B.C.) is credited with a "mid-dynasty restoration" (*zhong-xing*) of Zhou fortunes just before the Zhou state declined greatly when the former capital was attacked by non-Chinese tribes in 771 B.C. He accomplished this by ordering his various generals to carry out "northern punitive expeditions" (*bei-fa*) and "southern campaigns" (*nan-zheng*) against the various tribes that threatened the Zhou borders. These campaigns are recorded in four songs in the *Book of Songs*, included in Arthur Waley's translation in the "warriors and battles" section (nos. 133, 134, 136, and 139). Lu quite often alluded to King Xuan as the archetype of the kind of emperor he felt the Sung needed in order to defeat the Jin state and complete a Sung restoration.

The second couplet proclaims the theme "return my rivers and mountains" so common among Southern Sung patriots. Stylistically the lines are a perfect example of the verbal parallelism and tonal antithesis required of the two middle couplets in a Regulated Verse poem. Literally, the lines are, "four seas one family, Heaven-calendared number (of years); / two rivers hundred commanderies, Sung mountains waters (rivers)," (*si-hai yi-jia tian-li-shu; liang-he bo-jun song shan-chuan*). "Heaven-calendared number" refers to the Chinese political belief, originally a Zhou dynasty religiopolitical theory of legitimacy, that the mandate or fate (*ming*) of a dynasty is established by heaven (*tian*).

The third couplet, perfectly parallel and antithetical again, describes the tragic effects of the appeasement policy. "Brave warriors" (*zhi-shi*)—men with ambition, will, and determination to help the dynasty reconquer the lost territories, men like Lu himself, now fifty-eight years old—have "vainly wasted" (*xu-juan*, literally, "emptily dedicated") their services to the emperor without ever being sent off like King Xuan's generals to defeat the barbarian invaders and win back the lost lands. Rather, those lands of Jing and Lo, the Northern Sung capital cities of Bian-jing (Kaifeng) and Loyang, have been abandoned to alien hordes. Worst of all the "Great Emperor's tomb," the *Yong-chang-ling* ("Eternally fertile mound") of the Sung founder, Zhao Kuang-yin or Tai-zu ("Great Ancestor"), is overgrown and untended, as are the tombs of all of their ancestors. Surely, Lu pleads, this shameful situation should not be allowed to continue.

Ever since the earliest recorded times, Chinese scholars studied and wrote history as a mirror for their own day.[6] Lu You was also a historian as well as a poet, and from the last poem we can see that in his patriotic verse he constantly alluded to the heroes of the past whose martial exploits helped to establish great dynasties. True to the heroic tradition in Chinese literature and culture, it was the "spirit of justice" (*yi-qi*), courage, and individual freedom that he admired most about the warriors of the past. He did not demand that they all be victorious, and some of his favorite historical characters suffered tragic defeats.

The tragic hero who most captured his imagination was the same man whose life and fate Du Fu often brooded on—the prime minister of the Shu-Han kingdom during the Three Kingdoms period following the collapse of the Han dynasty, Zhu-ge Liang, styled Zhu-ge Kong-ming and also known as the Martial Marquis (*wu-hou*). This "quietest" wizard strategist of fiction and legend was just the sort of person that Lu could readily identify with, especially after his own dreams of reconquest were shattered and he was transferred to Chengdu. "Visiting the Martial Marquis Zhu-ge's Reading Terrace," a seven character Ancient Verse poem, was written in Chengdu in his fifty-second year and is a good example of his poems on Zhu-ge Liang.[7]

> Tall, tall, the grass on Gai-yang road;
> Sleeping Dragon long gone, empty remains his temple.
> Back then Si-ma was called a cunning bandit;
> 4 Courage lost, he dared not face the king's general.
> Before Bivouac Mountain on Cold Food road,
> To this day people worship at prime minister's tomb.
> Pine winds sound like his *Liang-fu Song*;
> 8 Remember how reluctantly he answered three visits.
> *Leading Troops,* unique memorial, thousand years unmatched,
> Far surpassing Guan Zhong and Le Yi of old.
> How can common scholars of today carry it out?
> 12 Those days in that lofty tower, what books were read?

Gai-yang (in modern Shaanxi province) is where Zhu-ge is said to have stationed troops during his attack on the kingdom of Wei. He is also said to have built a "reading terrace" (*du-shu-tai*) to attract the best scholars to the Shu-Han kingdom. He

was called a "sleeping dragon" (*wo-long*) by Xu Shu, the man
who introduced him to Liu Bei, king of Shu-Han and claimant
to the title of emperor as a descendant of the Liu family who
ruled the Han dynasty. The first couplet laments the fact that
Zhu-ge is gone and only his empty temple is left behind. Si-ma
Yi was a Wei general who refused to fight in single combat
when challenged by Zhu-ge. According to Zhu-ge's biography,
he ordered that his body be buried at "Bivouac Mountain"
(*ding-jun-shan*) in Gai county in Shaanxi. The Cold Food
Festival comes 105 days after the winter solstice and one or two
days before the Festival of Tombs and may be compared to Lent.[8]

The *Liang-fu Song* was a folk song that Zhu-ge Liang sang
as he peacefully tilled his fields in Nan-yang before entering
Liu Bei's service. The "pine winds" (*song-feng*), an image of
reclusion, here reminds Lu of Zhu-ge in his quiet seclusion.
Zhu-ge's natural inclinations, just like Lu's own inner feelings,
told him not to come out of his seclusion; and it was only
with the utmost "reluctance" (*fan-ran*, contrary to his better
judgment) that he "answered three visits" (*da-san-gu*) to his
grass hut from Liu Bei, who showed himself a true prince and
judge of men by waiting patiently in the freezing cold for an
audience with the already legendary Zhu-ge. *Leading Troops*
(*chu-shi-biao*) is a memorial that Zhu-ge wrote to express his
loyalty to Liu Bei's son and his plan of attack after Liu Bei's
death. Lu writes that it far surpasses the strategies of the great
military leaders of the Warring States period. Finally, Lu asks,
how can the goal of leading troops out to attack the north be
carried out today? In the last couplet, then, Lu seems to imply
that the "common scholars" (*su-ru*) of his day are not capable
of leading troops the way Zhu-ge Liang did because they no
longer study military strategy and tactics. Lu himself would
like to follow Zhu-ge's example, but he does not know what
books Zhu-ge read and taught in his reading terrace.

Another type of poem in the heroic mode that Lu excelled
in was the "border style" of Music Bureau (*yue-fu*) poems.
These poems generally describe drinking, riding, and hunting
on the borders, in preparation for an attack on alien tribes or
as training and discipline for the soldiers guarding the far
frontiers. The diction is usually full of martial images and

hyperbolic expressions of the "élan" (*qi*) of the courageous warriors.

The Han dynasty Music Bureau was the office responsible for supplying the music required by the court on various ceremonial occasions. Some of the later collections, all called *yue-fu* songs or ballads, contain military and ceremonial dance tunes as well as many popular or semipopular folk songs. After the collapse of the dynasty, the music was lost, but the titles and many texts remain to this day. Poets of the Tang dynasty, especially Li Bo, Du Fu, and Cen Shen, liked to write poems using *yue-fu* titles and alluding to Han dynasty events as a form of comment on and criticism of their own times.

Another reason poets such as Li Bo liked to use the *yue-fu* style was its freedom from the metrical restraints of the Regulated Verse form. During his middle period, Lu also enjoyed this freedom and wrote a number of *yue-fu* style poems employing varying line lengths and rhyme schemes. "Huns Have No Heroes," written at age forty-eight, is another of the best known of Lu's patriotic poems. It is basically a seven character Ancient Verse poem, but it also uses both five and three character lines for variation.[9]


        Beard like porcupine bristles,
        Face like angular quartz,
        A man strides forth, disdains ten thousand miles,
  4  Seizes at once his wind-cloud chance.
        Chase them fleeing, sleep 'neath dewy Blue Sea moon!
        Storm their cities, tread darkly Yellow River ice!
        Iron mail crosses stones: rain sighs softly.
  8  War drums ascend hilltop: thunder rumbles deeply.
        Midnight: beaten barbarians meekly offer surrender.
        Day dawns: their piled armor, hill upon hill.
        Middle Kingdom first knows blood-sweating steeds.
 12  Eastern tribes again present frost-feathered eagles.
        Dark hosts prostrate,
        Bright sun ascendant!
        Huns have no heroes,
 16  Sung flourishes anew!
        A true man having repaid his master thus,
        Would laugh at this white-headed old scholar.

As in so many of Lu's Ancient Verse poems, the narrative of this poem is presented through a series of four line segments. The first four lines describe the Confucian hero, the *zhang-fu*, whose awesome visage, bristling beard, and angular features must surely bring fear to the hearts of his enemies. He strides forth resolutely, thinking nothing of the great distances he must travel in order to do battle with the border tribes harassing his country. He seizes at once his "wind-cloud chance" (*feng-yun zhi hui*), an amazing concatenation of circumstances, mentioned in the *Book of Changes,* when the dragon clouds and tiger winds come together. "Clouds follow the dragon, winds follow the tiger," says the *Changes,* and both are powerful symbols of the Chinese military leader.[10]

In the next four line sequence Lu imagines the battle is joined with the "Huns" (*hu*, a general term for northern and western tribes since the Han dynasty, meaning here, of course, the Jürched). The Chinese heroes chase them both northward and westward as far as the desert wastes of Kokonor (*qing-hai*, "Blue Sea") and beyond the cold northern reaches of the Yellow River. The sound of the Chinese armored troops on the march is likened to the fury of a great thunderstorm. Although this is an Ancient Verse poem, these four lines form two perfectly balanced seven character parallel couplets. This parallelism even in poems not strictly requiring it is a distinctive characteristic of Lu's style, and an attempt has been made to capture this feature in the translation.

In the third four line sequence, also two balanced seven character couplets, Lu again employs Han and Tang dynasty allusions to describe the surrender of the barbarians and the victory of Chinese imperial might. "Middle Kingdom" (*zhong-hua,* "Central Floriate Kingdom"), familiar from recent newspaper accounts, is the ancient name for the Chinese homeland, revived by twentieth century nationalists in the name both for the Republic of China (Nationalist) and for the People's Republic of China (Communist). "Blood-sweating steeds" (*han-xue ma*), meaning the powerful Central Asian horses also known as "thousand-*li* horses" (*qian-li-ma*), were first captured from border tribes by the famous Han dynasty "Flying General" Li Guang (d. 119 B.C.), who is said to have stolen such a horse in order to escape when captured by the Xiong-nu.[11] As in the works of his friend Xin Qi-ji (1140–1207), allusions to Li Guang also abound in Lu's middle period poetry. "Frost-featherd eagles" (*shuang-mao-ying*), rare white eagles, were presented as tribute to the Tang court by the peoples of China's northeast borders.[12]

The fourth sequence consists of four three character lines that bring the poem to a crescendo with a great paean of victory. The two couplets also present a vivid contrast between the Chinese and the barbarians. The Jürched are a "dark host" (*qun-yin*), symbolic of everything negative and evil in the cosmic order, forced to "prostrate" (*fu*) themselves before the "great brightness" (*tai-yang*, the sun, as well as all the benevolent forces of the cosmos) of the Chinese empire "rising in the ascendant" (*sheng*) to herald a new dawn.[13] The "Huns have no heroes" (*hu wu ren*), literally, they are not even human, and the Sung empire "flourishes anew" (*zhong-xing*), experiencing a mid-dynastic restoration like that of the Zhou dynasty under King Xuan.

For patriots, this vision must be truly inspiring, but for Lu it only brought sorrow. In the final seven character couplet he returns from his dream to his own real life situation. He is sitting by his window writing by lamplight.[14] At forty-eight, and with an insignificant post in an out of the way place, he is about as far removed from the fighting hero of his vision as it is possible to be. Indeed, he laments, such a "true man" (*zhang-fu* again), having "repaid his master" (*bao-zhu*) for his benevolence by defeating the barbarians and regaining the lost lands for his emperor, would only laugh at Lu in derision.

I conclude this chapter with a group of poems in the heroic mode that are allegorical and highly imaginative rather than straightforwardly didactic. The first one, "Song of the Precious Sword," is ostensibly about a sword that longs to be employed against the barbarians; it is, however, a transparent symbol for the author, who at that point was a "secluded one" (*you-ren*) against his will. This five character Ancient Verse poem was also written when the poet was forty-eight and should be compared with the poem, "Expressing My Ambition," given below and written twenty-three years later.[15]

      Secluded one pillows head on precious sword;
      Twang! twang! resounds its nightly plaint.
      Some say swords can become dragons;
 4  Only fear evoking wind and thunder.
      Fiercely angry with crazed barbarians,
      It bravely longs for a far campaign.
      Rising, he pours libation to the sword:
 8  "The most precious should hide its form.
      Surely someone will acknowledge you.
      Your time come, you *will* be employed!
      One scabbard has plenty of room;
12  Why keep harping your discontent!"

The sword, like the poet himself, longs to go off and fight; but its time has not yet come. His libation to the sword expresses a common theme in Chinese literature. Someone possessing great talents ("most precious," *zhi-bao*) should not assert himself needlessly, but has only to bide his time like Jiang Tai-gong (fl. 1130 B.C.) or Zhu-ge Liang until a ruler who is also a true judge of men discovers him and gives him his chance to serve. Lu should be quite comfortable in his office in Sichuan and not keep "harping on his discontents" (*ming bu-ping*).

"Ballad of Pine and Warhorse," a seven character Ancient Verse poem written at age fifty in Chengdu during the period of his keenest frustration, expresses his feelings of unrestrained sadness, a side of his character different from that shown in his poems of drunken revelling with Fan Cheng-da.[16]

      Warhorse gallops a thousand *li* to achieve what?
      Head hanging at trough, ends by injuring itself.
      Pine watches a thousand years in abandoned river valley.
 4  Far better sacrifice itself to support the Bright Hall.
      Man is born embracing talents he wants to employ;
      Swears to take Yan-Zhao, return them to his king.
      Door closed, leisurely reclining, body growing older;
 8  Hearing chickens scratch about, tears streak my face.
      Were I to die in bed blubbering like a baby,
      Far better to stand tall braving battle field!
      Half-drunken flood-song resounds with fierce sadness,
12  Chariot wheels, a hundred turns, wrench anguished guts.

The first six lines express his frustration through the images of an old warhorse and an abandoned pine tree. The first couplet alludes to a *yue-fu* ballad by Cao Cao (155–220), the martial emperor of the Wei kingdom during the Three Kingdoms period. Cao's song was:

> Old warhorse leans at trough,
> Ambitious [to travel] a thousand *li*.
> Heroic warrior in twilight years,
> Brave heart not yet exhausted.

Du Fu also used this allusion and others in comparing himself to an old warhorse.[17] Lu often expressed the feeling that he was "injuring himself" (*zi-shang*) wandering around the empire serving in office. His sense of duty was stronger than his desire to escape at this time, however, and in the next couplet he rejects an idea he will later embrace. The pine (*song*) is usually a symbol of longevity and resistance, and the *Zhuang Zi* has many anecdotes teaching the usefullness of preserving one's body by being useless or "abandoned" (*qi*), by being a recluse and avoiding government service. Here, however, Lu writes that it would have been better for the pine to have been hewn down and made into timber to "support the Bright Hall" (*fu Ming-Tang*). The Bright Hall was a ceremonial hall built by the Han emperors to symbolize the entire universe, and it later came to stand for the Chinese Empire. A "man" (*shi*) is a "warrior" or a "scholar" and his vow, of course, is to return the lost northern lands (of Yan and Zhao, near modern Peking) to his king (*jun-wang*). The last half of the poem, then, elaborates on his great personal sadness as he lies in bed and feels himself growing older without having accomplished anything for the nation.

As Lu grew older he turned increasingly in the direction of Daoist quietism, but he never completely succeeded in forgetting the world, however hard he studied the *Zhuang Zi*. His great ambition remained the same as far as the nation was concerned. "Expressing My Ambition," a five character Ancient Verse poem written when he was seventy-one and living at home, is one of the finest examples of his blending of realistic descrip-

tion and sincere emotions—old age, weakness of body, poverty,
pride, and ambition—with romantic imagination—his self-trans-
formation into an avenging sword embued with divine magic.[18]

> Years ago leaving the capital gates,
> My retirement vow was firmly made.
> Today, willow-reed body
> 4   Suddenly reaches eighty!
> Wife and children tire of cold and hunger;
> Neighbor folk deride my vague clumsiness.
> I sing sadly while gathering grain;
> 8   Suppress anger while chewing snow.
> A thousand years buried under pine roots,
> Nether winds sweep over empty grave.
> Liver and heart alone not transformed,
> 12   Fuse together becoming iron and steel!
> Forged into a fine imperial sword,
> Sacrifice traitorous minister's blood!
> Sheathed up in military storage,
> 16   Or carried forth by vanguard troops.
> But three feet, far brighter than the stars;
> For a myriad miles pacifies ghosts and demons!
> Just looking at this divine marvel,
> 20   Ugly Huns seem hardly worth killing!

The first eight lines describe Lu's situation since retirement
by means of a number of very appropriate allusions. Wang Xi-
zhi (321–79), a famous calligrapher of the Jin dynasty who
lived in the Shao-xing area, once made a vow before his parents'
grave (*shi-mu*, "retirement vow") never to serve in office again.
"Willow-reeds" or "reed-willows" (*pu-liu*) dry up early in the
fall and had long been used to refer to the "appearance" (*zi*,
"body") of one who has become decrepit early in life. "Vague
clumsiness" (*yu-zhuo*) might well be translated "stubborn
eccentricity," for the term also has the connotation of the sort
of deliberate "ignorance" affected by the proud recluse. The next
two lines make this meaning explicit by alluding to two very
poor but very proud men who retained their integrity and self-
respect in great adversity. The *Lie Zi*, the *Tian-rui* chapter
("Heavenly Omens"), tells the following story: Lin Lei ("Forest
Species"), a Daoist recluse reputed to be over one hundred

years old, was walking along one day in his fields "singing a sad song" (*bei-ge*) and "gathering grain" (*shi-sui*), actually working with his own hands in a manner most unbecoming to the Confucian gentleman, when Confucius and his disciples passed near by. Confucius sent Zi Gong to talk to him. He asked Lin Lei if he were not sorry to be walking along working in the fields at his age, but Lin Lei simply ignored his question entirely and went proudly about his business.[19] When Su Wu (fl. 70 B.C.) was captured by the Xiong-nu, the Huns of the Han dynasty, they threw him into an icy pit to break his proud resistance; he lay there on the ground "chewing snow" (*nie-xue*) and refused to cooperate with his captors. From these allusions to proud resistance in poverty, old age and adversity, one Daoist and one Confucian, Lu turns to an imaginative fantasy of transformation and vengeance after his death.

Appropriately enough, he will be buried under a pine tree, his most often used symbol of endurance and resistance. After a thousand years his body will have mostly turned to dust, but his "liver and heart" (*gan-xin*), symbols of courage and loyalty, will be magically transformed into "iron and steel" (*jin-tie*). These hardy metals will then be forged into a "fine imperial sword" (*shang-fang jian*), a sword from the *Shang-fang*, the office of imperial clothing, bestowed by the emperor himself. Such a sword, wielded with two hands and able to cut a horse in half, was once requested of Han Cheng-di (r. 32–6 B.C.) by Zhu Yun who wanted it to kill a "traitorous minister" (*ning-chen*) at court. As such a magical sword, Lu would first take vengeance on the "traitorous ministers" he held responsible for the appeasement policy. Then he would go on to "pacify ghosts and demons" (*jing yao-nie*) everywhere around the empire, by which he surely means exterminate the "ugly Huns" (*chou-lu*), even though he claims they are "hardly worth killing."[20]

Lu continued to dream of a "northern expedition," and, when it finally came to pass under Han Tuo-zhou, he was elated at the beginning of the war. After the Sung defeat he continued to urge a prowar policy, but his urgings were increasingly written in the language of dreams, as if he knew in his heart that for him a reconquest could only take place in dreams. We have already seen that in his very last poem he urged his sons to remember him when the royal troops finally retook the northern territories. "A Strange Dream," a five character Regulated Verse poem written at age eighty-two, expresses his belief that even if he should die before that day there would certainly be a time when the Chinese would once more occupy the northern provinces of Yan and Zhao.[21]

> Had a strange dream in the mountains;
> In pleated armor brandished carved lance.
> Crossed the Wei River west of Shu Stream;
> 4   Attacked by Yellow River north of Tong Pass.
> Coldly, sadly, strummed the Zhao zithern;
> With lamentation sang the Yan songs.
> These things will one day come to pass;
> 8   It matters not that I age and die.

In conclusion we can say that Lu You's heroic and patriotic verse represents the most forceful, often strident, expression of the public side of his personality and thinking. In a language vivified by imaginative hyperbole, martial images, aptly chosen allusions, and skillfully balanced prosody, he created a body of fine poetry that represented a clarion call for war against the invaders of his homeland. His patriotism, then, was primarily an expression of pride in his own culture and way of life, as well as loyalty to the emperor as the symbol of both. It also included sympathy for the common people who made up the economic backbone of the nation. True to the heroic mode in Chinese poetry, many of these poems are full of unrestrained tears and sadness that sometimes borders on the maudlin. On the whole, however, they compel our admiration for the artistry with which they were written. It is not difficult to understand why this aspect of Lu's poetry has been consistently enjoyed and praised by his compatriots of all classes for the past eight hundred years.

### CHAPTER 4

# Recognitions of Transcendent Power: Daoism and Alchemy

IF Confucianism with its stress on duty and service to the state and nation was Lu You's public philosophy, Daoism was his personal philosophy. The Daoist tradition attracted him with its vision of individual freedom, liberation from the restraints of culture and society, the hope of longevity or even immortality, and the ideal of a primitive communal society characterized by political equality and social welfare. This chapter presents a selection from several hundred poems on Daoist themes, such as the use of psychedelic drugs, imaginative journeys in space, seclusion, divination, alchemy, and various hygienic practices, including meditation, all subsumed under the heading of "nuturing life" (*yang-sheng*).

Lu claimed that his family had been interested in alchemy for four generations. What this meant was that they had been engaged in the transmutation of base metals into gold, which was also believed to involve "the formation of *aurum non vulgi,* or the genesis of the homunculus, both of which symbolized the creation of fully conscious, cosmically oriented man."[1] They were not, of course, primitive smiths or merely superstitious mystics, but highly cultured men who were nevertheless very sympathetic to the "ancient wisdom" of China. They were, however, seeking physicial immortality. "Among the Daoists, whose alchemical furnace is successor to the ancient forge, immortality is no longer ... the result of the casting of a magic utensil ... but is acquired from him who has succeeded in producing the 'divine cinnabar.' From that moment there was a new means of self-deification; it was sufficient to absorb drinkable gold or cinnabar in order to become like the gods."[2] Lu's great-grandfather, Lu Zhen, was believed to have actually achieved

81

immortality through the practice of alchemy, and this fact had great influence on Lu's thinking. His *Colophon to the Mirror for Cultivating the Mind,* written at thirty-eight years of age, demonstrates his early belief in the possibility of attaining immortality.[3]

The above book, *Mirror for Cultivating the Mind,* in one chapter, was by my great-grandfather, the Grand Tutor. At first, when he was seven years old, his family was poor and he did not attend school. Suddenly he composed a poem on his own, using words of the holy immortals (*shen-xian*). Those who read it were astonished.

In his old age he styled himself the "Court Recluse" (*Chao Yin-Zi*). Once when he returned from court levee he saw an "extraordinary one" (an *yi-ren* or adept) walking in the air some three feet above the ground. He invited [my ancestor] to go with him. He was the ancient immortal of Mount Song. [Shi] Xi-zhen, also known as [Shi] Jian-wu. [My ancestor] received from him the techniques of "refining cinnabar [elixirs] and avoiding grains" (*lian-dan bi-gu*) and departed [i.e., became an immortal] by means of the method of "separation from the corpse" (*shi-jie*).

His techniques were kept secret and not transmitted and only this book has survived. Thus I have had it printed and transmitted to the world, at the end of the book appending the poem he wrote at seven and his self-appreciation. It is my sincere hope that those gentlemen who "roam beyond the realm" will gain some inspiration from reading this book. That was also my ancestor's wish.

Another anecdote about his family, written between the ages of sixty-seven and sixty-nine, attests to his abiding faith in the efficacy of Daoist medical practices and the existence of Daoist immortals.[4]

My grandmother, the Lady of Chu, was ill for several months in the capital during 1110. Even famous physicians like Shi Cang-yong all said she was very difficult to cure. One day an old Daoist, with a very ancient appearance, wearing a copper cap and a purple cloak trimmed with feathers, followed by a young boy with two tufts on his head and a white fan with a long handle in his hand, passed her door. He said that no matter how grave any sickness was, immediate recovery could be brought about by one simple cauterization. My late father invited him in and inquired about his skill (*shu*). The Daoist then produced a little moxa from his bag, took a piece of tile and started to cauterize it. My grandmother was then asleep. She suddenly felt great pain in her abdomen as if being burned by fire. [She was thus cured.]

The Daoist said that he was ninety years old. He left all of a sudden and went very fast so that no one following him could catch up. My grandmother was not yet sixty at the time. She lived for more than twenty years after that before she died at eighty-three.

Twenty years after my grandmother died, my cousin Zi-yi was supervising the salt farms at Three Rivers. Once while drinking with a certain scholar named Mao, they suddenly saw a Daoist. His general appearance and that of the boy [with him] seemed to coincide with the description my grandmother had previously given. While [they] were still startled, the Daoist himself suddenly told of the cauterization of the tile in the capital. After that he escaped and a search could not locate him. Mao then said that when his wife was ill a Daoist [the same one?] cured her instantly by cauterizing more than ten pillars in their house, but when he wanted to thank him he had unexpectedly gone away.

There are some in this world who doubt [the existence of] holy immortals (*shen-xian*), considering it to be far-fetched. How mistaken they are!

The first poem in this chapter, replete with alchemical allusions, seems to describe a meeting Lu had in Sichuan's Min and E-mei mountains with an old adept who gave him some kind of psychedelic drug. Scholars do not really know whether the Chinese used psychedelic drugs, and, if they did, what kinds they used; but Lu often mentions various herbs and describes them in a manner similar to psychedelics.[5] The drug had the usual effect of creating a euphoric sensation leading to a "trip" or imaginative journey similar to many we are familiar with from European and American writers. His feelings of elation on this occasion reached a point of ultimate transcendence— temporary, of course—in which the highest of the five sacred mountains, Mount Song in Henan (*qing-song*, "Green Mountain") appeared a mere "ant hill" (*yi-die*). "An Qi Chapter" is a five character Ancient Verse poem and was written when he was fifty-nine.[6]

> Long ago I roamed Mounts Min and E,
> Picking wisteria on thousand foot peaks.

An old man leaned on red rattan staff;
4   I suspect he was the Venerable An Qi.
He gave me a single elixir pill;
Five clouds emerged from his calabash.
But an instant after swallowing it,
8   Gem-bright became my ice-snow countenance!
Pure hands held mountain mists;
Black hair blown by heaven winds.
The old one, seeing my joy,
12   Shared a ride on his green dragon.
Never again search for Mystic Isles.
I loved that myriad mile void!
Passing back over the Central Continent,
16   Lofty Green Mountain seemed an ant hill!

"Venerable An Qi" (*An Qi Weng*), usually called Master An Qi, was a legendary Daoist who had attained physical immortality and lived on the "Mystic Isles" (*peng-lai*) in the eastern sea. He was said to have invited the first emperor, Qin Shi-huang-di (r. 221–209 B.C.), to visit him there. He refused to accept any money for his instruction to that monarch, but he left some magic artifacts behind at the Qin court. During Han Wu-di's (r. 149–86 B.C.) time, the adept Li Shao-jun claimed to have seen An Qi eating jujubes as large as melons.[7] The "five clouds" (*wu-yun*) that emerged from An Qi's "calabash" (*piao*) were auspicious omens, and the tradition associated with these clouds in the five colors of green, white, red, black, and yellow went back to at least the Zhou dynasty.[8] The Daoist's calabash was "regarded as representing the cosmos in miniature. In this gourd-shaped microcosm reside[d] the source of Life and Youth. This theme—the universe having the shape of a calabash— is of undeniable antiquity."[9] The "Central Continent" is literally Qi-zhou, anciently considered to be the most central of the nine island continents into which the world was believed to be divided; hence it stands for all of China.

"Kun-lun Journey," a seven character Ancient Verse poem, was written shortly after "An Qi Chapter" and is really an answer to it.[10]

Dark clouds cleave asunder, morning sun reddens;
Yellow River straight with far-off Kun-lun joins.

If not riding twin phoenixes, then yoking curled dragons.
4 Straightway I follow incense smoke ascending the void.
My journey suddenly passing Sun Moon Palace,
See below congealed vapors green misty haze.
Cold and heat undifferentiated, day and night the same,
8 High and rugged the Nine Gates with frequent fierce winds.
Bitter cold, dark desolation becoming melted and diffused,
Neither agitated nor dizzy, my body feels quite empty.
Dust and sand for numberless aeons revolve without end,
12 Why bother then further seeking the Venerable An Qi!

A quotation from Mircea Eliade's *The Forge and the Crucible* may serve as a commentary for this remarkably symbolic poem.[11]

But cinnabar can also be made inside the human body, mainly by means of the distillation of sperm. "The Daoist, imitating animals and vegetables, hangs himself upside down, causing the essence of his sperm [Yellow River of line 2] to flow up to his brain." The *dantian*, the "famous fields of cinnabar," are to be found in the most secret recesses of the brain and belly: there it is that the embryo of immortality is alchemically prepared. Another name for these "cinnabar fields" is *Kun Lun*, meaning both "mountain of the western sea"—a sojourn of the immortals—and a secret region of the brain, comprising the "chamber similar to a cave" (*dong-fang*, which also signifies "nuptial chamber") and the "nirvana" (*ni-wan*). "In order to enter therein by mystic meditation, one falls into a 'chaotic' state (*hun*) resembling the primordial, paradisal, 'unconscious' condition of the uncreated world."

Although Lu seems to have sometimes sampled psychedelics, as in the "An Qi Chapter," just as he often got very drunk on home-brewed wine, throughout most of his life, and especially as he grew older, he was an advocate of the "inner hygiene" (*nei-dan*) school of thought. He believed that the ingestion of "external substances" (*wai-wu*) such as herbals or elixirs (*yao*) and wine (*jiu*), however pleasant, was not the proper way to achieve enlightenment. He believed instead in "nurturing the psychic energies" (*yang-qi*) through quiet meditation. This poem, then, is a symbolic description of a journey *through* the mind (a la William Blake) or *beyond* the mind (as the *Zhuang Zi* advocated) back to the "primordial, paradisal, 'unconscious' condition of the uncreated world" wherein Lu achieved enlightenment through the realization that the universe just goes on and he need no longer seek for spiritual advice from gurus like An Qi.

The realization that Lu arrived at, however temporarily again, is well described in this quotation from Alan Watts's *Psychotherapy East and West*.[12]

The point is not that the [so-called] problem [of life] has no solution, but that it is so meaningless that it *need not be felt as a problem*. To quote Wittgenstein again:

> For an answer which cannot be expressed the question too cannot be expressed. *The riddle does not exist.* If a question can be put at all, then it *can* also be answered. . . . For doubt can only exist where there is a question; a question only where something can be *said*. We feel that even if all possible scientific questions be answered, the problems of life have still not been touched at all. Of course *there is then no question left, and just this is the answer.* The solution of the problem of life is seen in the vanishing of this problem. (Is not this the reason why men to whom after long doubting the sense of life became clear, could not then say wherein this sense consisted?)

In his poems concerning meditation, Lu often refers to the "morning sun" (*zhao-dun*), once symbolically as a vision seen at midnight,[13] and I believe that the first two lines of this poem picture him deep in meditation at dawn on his mat before an incense burner. His trance has reached a high point and he feels that the "Yellow River" (*huang-he*), symbolic of his essence or sperm (the same term, *jing*, in Chinese), "joins" (*tong*) with the Kun-lun Mountains, symbolic of his brain. He imagines himself then taking off into the "void" (*kong*), being pulled either by "twin phoenixes" (*luan-feng*) or "curled dragons" (*qiu-long*), favorite mounts of the immortals. *Luan, feng,* and *long* are all symbolic of divine powers for the Chinese, and refer here to the Goethian "wings of the spirit" upon which Lu feels himself to be lifted beyond the mundane world of the mind's normal and culturally limited perception.

His imaginative journey takes him as high as the "Sun Moon Palace" (*ri-yue-gong*, apparently his own invention), from which vantage point he can look down on the not yet created world. He has reached in his mind the "undifferentiated"(*bu-*

*fen*) state of the primordial unconscious—that is, he has reached
the state in which he sees with his "spirit" (*yi-shen*) like the
*Zhuang Zi's* Cook Ding and no longer perceives with his culturally limited mind the supposed separation between subject
and object, between "inner" and "outer." He feels with the
*Zhuang Zi* that "Heaven and Earth were born together with me
and the myriad things are one with me," and he has found,
like Goethe, that there is "Nothing 'inside' or 'out there,'/The
'outer' world is all 'In Here.' "[14]

It is this escape from or transcendence of the feeling of
differentiation of ego and object (or organism and environment)
that constitutes the "liberation" or "enlightenment" of Daoism
and Chan Buddhism. Modern physical science has taught us in
twentieth century Europe and America what the Daoist and Chan
Buddhists knew (or felt intuitively) long ago—that there are no
such things as space, force, and matter, but "only the *unity* of
certain *functional relations*"; that there can be no meaningful
discussion of an organism apart from an environment and vice
versa; that the world is in fact a field of organism-environment
interrelations. As Watts argues so well, Daoist or Chan liberation
or enlightenment "has nothing to do with a perception of something else than the physical world. On the contrary, it is *the
clear perception of this world as a field,* a perception which is
not just theoretical but which is also *felt* as clearly as we feel,
say that 'I' am a thinker behind and apart from my thoughts, . . .
When this *relativity of things* is seen very strongly [as with Lu
You here, with what Wordsworth called "undisordered sight"],
its appropriate effect is love rather than hate or fear."[15]

Having thus without the aid of drugs reached this new perception of the universe as an undifferentiated field,[16] Lu then imaginatively passes through the "Nine Gates" (*jiu-guan*) of
Heaven, said to be guarded by fierce tigers and leopards who
devour those mortals who aspire to enter therein.[17] That is to say,
he reaches enlightenment through his intense concentration and
despite all of the obstacles that distract the mind (symbolized
by the tigers and leopards), and his enlightenment is followed
by a feeling of great peace. His "bitter cold, dark desolation"
(*lin-ran xiao-sen*), alienation, "becomes melted and diffused"
(*bian chong-rong*) in a floodlike feeling of cosmic ataraxy. Like

Dante coming out of purgatory or Tripitaka crossing the great
river into Buddhaland (in the Chinese novel *Monkey*), "neither
agitated nor dizzy" (*bu-ji bu-xuan*) any longer, his "body feels
quite empty" (*shen ru kong*) and light. From travelling in the
Void (*kong*) he has become one with it, he has become void
(*kong*, empty, nothing) himself, and, thus, his "language is the
language not of reason but love [and poetry]. . . . Love comes
emptyhanded; the eternal proletariat; like Cordelia, bringing
Nothing."[18] He realizes that life is not a problem, that there are
no problems in nature, that in nature "dust and sand" (*chen-
sha*), Buddhist terms for objects of sense perception that are
"numberless as the atoms") for "numberless aeons" (*hao-jie*, a
*jie* being a Hindu-Buddhist *kalpa*, an extremely long time)
"revolve without end" (*huan wu-qiong*).[19] Having reached this
high state of understanding, he no longer has any need to seek
the venerable Daoist immortal An Qi. In light of the poem "An
Qi Chapter," I feel that he is also saying symbolically that one
need not use psychedelic drugs to achieve enlightenment.

Lu's feeling of enlightenment and liberation at the age of
fifty-nine was not a permanent feeling that resulted in any
remarkable and lasting change in his personality, however, and he
did continue to study alchemy in preparation for making the
Great Elixir. Since the making of the elixir must be done in
seclusion and with great secrecy, Lu had to wait until after
he had retired at the age of sixty-four to embark on his experiments. "Ballad of Avoiding the World," written three years
later in a very free Ancient Verse style to match the desire for
freedom expressed, describes very clearly his relief at being
retired from office and finally able to satisfy his often-expressed
desire to "avoid the world" (*bi-shi*).[20]

> When thirsty you do not drink deadly henbane.
> When hungry you do not eat black nightshade.
> Due solely to your clear discernment,
> 4　Acceptance or rejection need no deliberation.
> My eyes look up to the blue skies;
> I've so little joy greeting guests.
> My mouth savors only pine nuts;
> 8　Cooked food's too much trouble.

> Taking office to support wife and children,
> How could I have avoided falling into a trap?
> Knives, swords, kettles, cauldrons—
> All those instruments of torture—
> 12  Did I not bring down upon myself?
> I want to find a place where human feet have never trod,
> Forget my body, utterly vanish among wild hart and hind.
> Atop a green cliff secretly secluded among white clouds,
> 16  Live in a nest a thousand years forever avoiding the world!

The first four lines compare taking office to deliberately eating deadly poisons and assert that a person should know whether to "accept or reject" (*qu-she*) such action due to human intelligence. The next four lines state that he not only rejects official life but that he also finds little pleasure in any sort of social intercourse and is ready to live on "pine nuts" (*song-bo*) like a Daoist hermit. In the next four lines he recalls that he fell into the trap of taking office, as did his model Tao Yuan-ming, due to the economic necessity of supporting a family. Thus he brought all that pain and torture down upon himself. At this point he has conveniently forgotten that he also took office because of his great desire for "merit and fame" (*gong-ming*). Now, however, he is retired and free to do what he had wanted to do for so long—to live in seclusion and to explore the alchemical secrets of immortality.

"Forget my body" (*wang-xing*) is an allusion to an anecdote in the *Zhuang Zi,* Chapter twenty-eight, concerning Confucius's disciple Zeng Zi living as an impoverished Daoist recluse.[21]

> The Son of Heaven could not get him for his minister; the feudal lords could not get him for their friend. Hence he who nourishes his will forgets his bodily form (*yang-zhi-zhe wang-xing*); he who nourishes his bodily form forgets about questions of gain [profit]; and he who arrives at the Way forgets about his mind.

In retirement, then, Lu is saying that he will "nourish his will" and his integrity. He will return into the bosom of nature and imitate the birds by "living in a nest" (*chao-ju*), just as the old Daoist of Sichuan, Shang-guan Dao-ren, had done, and just as the people who lived in the age of primordial communality had done. The *Zhuang Zi*, Chapter twenty-nine, describes them thus:[22]

Moreover, I have heard [said Robber Zhi to Confucius] that in ancient times the birds and beasts were many and the people few. Therefore the people all nested in the trees in order to escape danger, during the day gathering acorns and chestnuts, at sundown climbing back up to sleep in their trees. Hence they were called the people of the Nest-builder. In ancient times the people knew nothing about wearing clothes. In summer they heaped up great piles of firewood; in winter they burned them to keep warm. Hence they were called "the people who know how to stay alive." In the age of Shen Nong [legendary inventor of agriculture], the people lay down peaceful and easy, woke up wide-eyed and blank. They knew their mothers but not their fathers [remarkable anthropological insight here], and lived side by side with the elk and the deer. They plowed for their food, wove for their clothing, and had no thought in their hearts of harming one another. This was Perfect Virtue at its height!

Lu's Daoist-inspired view of the superiority of the societies of the primordial past should not, I feel, be interpreted and then dismissed as an impossible "double longing after innocence and happiness."[23] Rather, it provides a thoroughgoing critique of archaic (whether feudal or semifeudal) and modern industrial (whether capitalist or communist or something in between) civilizations, and is a view that is fully shared by at least one leading anthropologist. Stanley Diamond writes,[24] "If the fulfillment and delineation of the human person within a social, natural, and supernatural (self-transcendent) setting is a universally valid measure for the evaluation of culture, primitive societies are our primitive superiors ... in the basic and essential respects ... primitive societies illuminate, by contrast, the dark side of a world civilization which is in chronic crisis."

Such primitive societies, as Diamond describes them and as the Daoists who wrote the *Zhuang Zi* and the *Lao Zi* "remembered" them, "rest on a communalistic economic base," rely on "communal and traditional, not political or secular" leadership, have no "laws, as we know them," "change slowly" and "do not manifest the internal turbulence endemic in archaic [e.g., Lu You's China] or contemporary civilizations," allow for a "very high degree of integration among the various major modalities

of culture," permit the "ordinary member" of society to partici-
pate "in a much greater segment of his social economy than do
individuals in archaic, and in technically sophisticated, modern
societies," are "holistic and moral, but not moralistic" in character [precisely what the *Lao Zi* means when it asserts that
human beings were naturally moral *until* they knew about
"morality" (*ren-yi dao-de*), the primary Confucian virtues],[25]
and practiced a "ritual drama" in which "art, religion, and daily
life" fused in "a culturally comprehensive vehicle for group and
individual expression at critical junctures in the social round
or personal life cycle, as these crises are enjoined by the natural
environment or defined by culture."[26]

Lu You certainly felt deeply alienated from many trends in
his society, as witness his preference for rural over urban life,
and he sought seclusion in order to retire to his "Daoist
Laboratory" (*dao-shi*) and practice the alchemical arts. Sometimes in his seclusion he compared himself to Daoist hermits
out of the *Zhuang Zi* and felt that he had found his immortality
in the world of men and in nature. This feeling is expressed
in "Seeking Plum Blossoms on Lakeside Hills," a seven character
Regulated Verse poem written at the age of eighty-three.[27]

> Mirror Lake, distant, cloudy, its misty ripples white,
> Is not joined to the human world's earthly waterways.
> Dragon-riding ancient immortal rejects fired food.
> 4  Habitually dwells in empty hills eating icy snow.
> Eastern Brightness, so lofty, beyond normal thought,
> Just like Chao and Xu living among mortal men.
> Myriad trees stiffly dead, but I alone survive.
> 8  In essence, immortality *is not* the soul's return!

This poem begins with a description of his earthly surround-
ings, rises through a series of metaphors and allusions to a kind
of self-deification, and then returns to announce his immortality
in nature. The first couplet describes the area around Mirror
Lake near his home in the late winter. An other-worldly mood
is created in the first line by the use of the words "distant,"
"cloudy," and "misty" (*miao-miao* and *yan*). This makes it easy
for us to believe that the spot "is not joined to the human
world's earthly waterways." Thus it is the perfect place for a

"dragon-riding ancient immortal" (*qi-long gu-xian*) to live in seclusion surviving on uncooked foods and snow.

The third couplet greatly enlarges the stature of the "ancient immortal." "Eastern Brightness" (*dong-huang*) was the title of a supreme deity of the state of Chu, the original homeland of the Lu family, as well as a star spirit; and was also known as the "Eastern Brightness Great Unique" (*tai-yi*).[28] "Chao and Xu" are Chao Fu ("Nest Father") and Xu You ("Promise of Freedom"), two legendary recluse sages during the reign of the Sage Emperor Yao. Xu You appears repeatedly in the *Zhuang Zi* and is most noted for rejecting the empire when Yao wanted to cede it to him. He replied to Yao's request: ". . . Go home and forget the matter, my lord. I have no use for the rulership of the world!"[29] In these two lines, then, Lu compares himself to a god of Chu, understanding of whom is "beyond normal thought" (*zhi du-wai*) as well as to transcendent sages dwelling among ordinary men.

In the final couplet he again describes the scene around him as he looks at the trees stripped bare by the winter cold and looking as if "stiffly dead" (*jiang-si*) and feels, in his bodily warmth as he trudges through the snow looking for plum blossoms, that "I alone survive" (*wo du-cun*) the rigors of winter. The winter may be regarded as symbolic of the last years of his life with its attendant illness and poverty, just as the plum blossoms, his favorite phenomenon of nature, may be regarded as symbolic of his resistance. The "soul's return" (*fan-hun*) refers to the belief of the "external hygiene" (*wai-dan*) schools of Daoism that the soul could return and dwell immortal on this earth after the ingestion of various "soul-returning herbs, grasses, or cinnabar elixirs" (*fan-hun-cao, yao,* or *dan*). The last line joyfully rejects these ideas and implies that "immortality" (*chang-sheng*), perhaps only "longevity," is not to be found in the soul's return after death, but rather is to be found by living naturally in the woods and never leaving. Returned into the bosom of nature, seeking for his favorite plum blossoms, he is truly the enlightened one.

In his Daoist poems, Lu alluded to quite different people than in his patriotic verse. "Ge Hong, or Affairs Beyond this World," a five character Ancient Verse poem written at the

age of seventy-nine, demonstrates his desire to follow his alchemical mentors.[30] Ge Hong (254–334), whose style was
Zhi-chuan, is one of the best known of many neo-Daoist al-
chemists of the North-South dynasties period. According to his
biography in the *Jin-shu*, he received his alchemical training
from Zheng Yin, also called Si-yuan, who was himself a disciple
of Ge Hong's great-uncle Ge Xuan ("The Mysterious"). He
was very poor and very studious and, after exploring every
facet of Daoist alchemy and receiving both written and secret
oral instruction, he wrote his great work, the *Bao Pu-zi*, which
may be translated "Embracing the Uncarved Block" (following
the late Arthur Waley) or "Book of the Preservation-of-Solidarity"
(following Joseph Needham). This small volume, which Lu
considered "more than enough to save the world" (*du-shi gai
you-yu*), is divided into two parts. The first twenty chapters,
collectively entitled the *Inner Chapters* (*nei-pian*), deal with
the preparation of alchemical elixirs, gold, longevity, and immortality, and are of major importance for the study of Chinese
alchemy. The last fifty chapters, the *Outer Chapters* (*wai-pian*),
are primarily concerned with social and political matters and
contain many radical ideas.[31] Ge Hong sought an official position
below the rank he was entitled to in order to obtain cinnabar
in Annam, he claims to have successfully refined the Great
Elixir of Immortality, and his biography records that he became
an immortal through the same "escape from the corpse" method
used by Lu's great-grandfather, thus leaving behind only his
clothes.

> Zhi-chuan learned from Master Zheng,
> Produced only one slim volume.
> A scroll the size of a chopstick—
> 4 More than enough to save the world.
> Ponder his discussions and explanations,
> Mysterious beyond Xuan and Hao's beginnings.
> *Inner Chapters* remain beside me today,
> 8 Again serving as food for bookworms.
> I want to explore their original secrets;
> With halting gait vainly stumble along.
> How can I attach a pair of wings,
> 12 Roam the Great Void with the Master!

As the many references to Ge Hong and the *Bao Pu-zi* throughout his poetry attest, Lu often read and studied this work. It probably served as the primary text for his alchemical experiments. It is an extremely esoteric and difficult book, however, and we can hardly blame him for feeling rather discouraged with his very slow progress, despite his great desire to master the mysterious arts. The book, he says, is so "mysterious" (or "wondrous," "marvelous" *miao*) that it takes one back to the time before the birth of the Yellow Ancestor (Huang Di or Xuan) and his son Shao Hao of the third millenium B.C. The Yellow Ancestor was reported to be responsible for the banishment of many of the "legendary rebels" that Needham believes were "the leaders of that prefeudal collectivist society which resisted transformation into feudal or proto-feudal class-differentiated society."[32] Lu often looked back to the prefeudal, pre-imperial society of Daoist communalism as a possible solution to the social problems of Sung China, and perhaps he understood Ge Hong's social message in the way that Needham sees it. At this point, however, the effort of understanding is too much for the old man and he vainly wishes for a "pair of wings" such as the immortals of old had in order to "roam the Great Void" (*you tai-xu*) with Ge Hong. The *Tai-xu* is mentioned in the *Zhuang Zi*, Chapter twenty-eight, in a passage describing the great difficulty of understanding the mysterious and formless Way (*Dao*): "Such men [who ask or answer questions about the *Dao*] can never trek across the Kun-lun, can never wander in the Great Void."[33] This allusion expresses Lu's admiration for the *Bao Pu-zi* by comparing it to the *Dao*, as well as expressing his own great difficulty in trying to understand the unfathomable.

"Nurturing Life," a five character Ancient Verse poem written when he was seventy-eight, is typical of his poems on the theme of various hygienic practices known as "nurturing life" (*yang-sheng*).[34]

> Innate constitution originally was not strong;
> Already at forty suddenly grew infirm.
> Medicine bag never left my hands;
> 4  Could not eat sweetmeats with wine.

Would never imagine today at eighty,
Still some black hairs among the white.
Although biting and chewing is somewhat difficult,
8  Happily not yet gumming cud like a cow.
Although formerly I studied nurturing life,
I rarely encountered any eminent masters.
Since gold and cinnabar are so obscure,
12  How can I hope for phoenix and crane?
There's only the Cook Ding chapter
To believe without the slightest doubt.
Love your body more than precious jade,
16  Polish it to avoid any fault or blemish.
Do not fear Heaven-sent calamities;
Only worry about self-caused distress.
Crooked and crippled you feel great pain,
20  But affliction is still in your four limbs.
Demons of illness invading your vital regions,
Even the finest physicians cannot cure you.
For cap and clothing observe the heat or cold;
24  In food and drink be ruled by hunger or thirst.
Even though tigers and rhinos be right beside you,
How can they use their horns or claws?
An old man not talking foolishness,
28  Thus I write this life-nourishing poem.

Lu's prescription for "nurturing life" is something that nearly every Chinese believed in and practiced as a matter of course, and most Chinese over forty still practice it. Basically it amounts to nothing more complicated than practicing moderation in all one's daily life activities, something that Confucianism with its middle way also advocated. One should avoid self-inflicted "distress" or "anxiety" ( *qi* ) and not worry about Heaven-sent "calamities" ( *nie* ) that one can do little to avoid anyway. What a person can do is to care for his body as he would a "precious jade" ( *gong-bi,* a highly valued jade ceremonial object), by maintaining a disciplined concentration in all things so that it becomes second nature, as did butchering oxen for King Hui's Cook Ding. Wear clothing that is suitable for the weather, and eat and drink moderately and only when actually responding to hunger or thirst, not compulsively or as social entertainment. This is the Chan (Zen) master's famous definition when asked

what was the discipline of Chan and wherein he differed
from most people.[35]

"When I am hungry I eat; when tired I sleep." "This is what
everybody does," insisted the questioner. "No," replied the master,
"because when they eat they do not eat, but are thinking of various
other things, thereby allowing themselves to be disturbed; when
they sleep they do not sleep, but dream of a thousand and one things.
This is why they are not like myself."

The "tigers and rhinos" (*hu-si*) are symbolic of the many
temptations to excess that could cause imbalance and illness if
one relaxed his discipline and gave in to them.

Although Lu was sometimes disillusioned by his attempts
to refine alchemical elixirs and, during moods of depression,
wrote of his frustration and fear,[36] in general his attitude toward
"the Work" was serious and optimistic. "Revealing My Thoughts
in the Daoist Laboratory," a seven character regulated poem
written at the age of seventy-eight, demonstrates his preference
for meditation and quieting the mind over the use of alchemical
elixirs.[37]

> To nuture mind work diligently at returning to
>     the child,
> Be willing to have not the smallest foolish desire.
> Mad Daoist adept in two inch grass hat.
> 4  Old style scholar with one volume wormy book.
> Fox fairies follow you standing like women.
> Gold's value with me cheap as dirt.
> Always suspect Bent Mountain's too near to
>     court and market—
> 8  Next year I'll ascend the gorges, visit Mount
>     Green Wall.

The first couplet of this poem describes "nurturing the mind"
(*yang-xin*) as the practice of breathing exercises, the primary
purpose of which was "to try to return to the manner of
respiration of the embryo in the womb [*huan-ying*, my "returning
to the child"]. Knowing nothing of the gases in the maternal
and foetal circulations, this could have been for the Daoists

but a fantasy; they tried to keep the inspiration and expiration as quiet as possible, and, above all, to hold the breath closed up (*bi-qi*) for as long as possible. There can be little doubt that the subjective effects which they experienced, and which they believed were so good for them, were due largely to anoxaemia, since they experienced asphyxic symptoms, buzzing in the ears, vertigo, and sweating."[38] Lu also experienced on several occasions visions of a "divine light" (*shen-guang*) emanating from his eyes and of the "morning sun" (*dun*) rising at midnight. A further goal of these exercises, the effects of which were no doubt of most benefit to the health, was to calm the mind and heart (same word, *xin*, in Chinese) and to lessen the desires; in short, to relax bodily tensions.

The second couplet again paints two self-portraits, now as the eccentric (*kuang*, "mad / madcap, wild, crazy") Daoist adept wearing a peasant style grass rain hat, and then as an old scholar poring over his "one volume wormy book" (*yi-ben du-jian*), perhaps the *Manual of Embryonic Respiration* (*tai-xi-jing*) or the *Bao Pu-zi*. The third couplet describes some of the temptations that surround him or anyone else seeking to lessen desire and nurture the spiritual side of his nature. "Fox fairies" (*hu-yao*) usually appear in the guise of beautiful women who try to lead men to hell and may be regarded here as symbolic of the temptations of the flesh. Gold, symbolizing the greedy desire for "profit" (*li*), which was strongly denounced in such orthodox Confucian texts as the *Analects* and the *Mencius,* is one temptation that Lu had long since overcome.

 Living as he did in Shao-xing county not far from Hangzhou, all of the various temptations of the "court and market place" (*chao-shi*), not the least of which was his still smoldering desire to serve the nation and establish merit, were too close for comfort. Even "Bent Mountain" (*Gou-qu-shan*) in Jiangsu, where Huang Chu-ping lived in seclusion, is "suspect" (*xian*) as being too near these urban temptations. It would be far better, he concludes, to go deeper into seclusion and away from these heavily populated regions by "ascending the [Sichuan] gorges to visit Mount Green Wall" where he had long ago met the venerable Shang-guan Dao-ren. Once more Lu emphasizes the need to return into nature in order to find peace.

A fitting conclusion to this chapter is one of Lu's latest poems, "Resting by the North Window in the Heat of the Day," a five character Ancient Verse poem written at the age of eighty-two, which provides a narrative summation of his life experiences in nurturing life, preventing illness, meditation, and seeking transcendent enlightenment.[39]

> Preventing illness is like controlling rivers,
> You only have to channel them eastward,
> Flowing seaward they find repose,
> 4 Naturally following earth's contours.
> Nurturing life is like growing trees,
> Cultivation and care must be suitable.
> Always striving to prevent serious injury,
> 8 In time they'll naturally touch the clouds.
> In youth I suffered many illnesses,
> Was several times in great danger.
> Bright Heaven certainly saw this;
> 12 Its warning message I still recall:
> "Middle years reject harmful desires;
> Late years regulate food and drink.
> Firmly centered, decline external temptations;
> 16 Though demons flourish, practice *Samadhibala*."
> Though life and death follow nature's design,
> Men and environments always mutually interact.
> In the midst of life's many vast roadways,
> 20 A hundred calamities arise from one desire.
> Warm rain falling on country village,
> Off come my headband and my socks.
> Leisurely reclining in north window's coolness,
> 24 Such broad awareness brings me transcendence!

The first four lines are an extended metaphor in which the prevention of illness is compared to the work of the great Yu, reputed to have lived in nearby Kuai-ji, who ended the Chinese flood when he "channelled" (*dao*) all of the rivers in China so that they would naturally flow eastward to the sea. Lu believed that illness, an imbalance in the human body analogous to a flood in nature, could be cured by quiet (*jing*) meditation (*zuo*) that allowed nature to restore the balance. In the next four lines, "nurturing life" (*yang-sheng*) is compared to the correct "cultivation and care" (*pei-zhi*) of trees in another extended metaphor very similar to the famous story of Ox Mountain in the *Mencius*. Relating how the mountain was stripped of its beautiful trees and fine meadowlands, just as man's spiritual strength is dissipated, Mencius concluded, "given the right nourishment (*yang*) there is nothing that will not grow, and deprived of it there is nothing that will not wither away."[40]

The next few lines relate how in his youth Lu suffered from many illnesses and frequently had to rely on medicine until he learned the virtue of moderation from what he regarded as a heaven-sent warning. All of us tend to forget past faults as we grow older, and Lu was no exception. His "middle years" (*zhong-nian*), which included his reckless abandon in Chengdu in his late forties and early fifties, are now seen as a time when he learned to "reject harmful desires" (*qi shi-yu*). In his "late years" (*wan-sui*), literally hundreds of poems attest to the fact that he did indeed "regulate food and drink (*jie yin-shi*), except, of course, for an occasional drinking bout. He practiced meditation to build up his spiritual center (*zhong-jian*, "centering firmly" to achieve perfectly relaxed concentration) and to avoid "external temptations" (*wai-mu*). Although these temptations, like "demons" (*muo*), "flourished in great numbers" (*sheng*) all about him, his meditation reached the stage of complete imperturbability that the Buddhists called *Samadhibala* (*ding-li*, "resolute power" in Chinese)—"the power of abstract or ecstatic meditation, [and the] ability to overcome all disturbing thoughts."[41]

Thus he had come to understand that all of the "hundred calamities" (*bai-huo*) of life are caused by "one desire" (*yi-tan*), by man's desireful nature running to excess. Perhaps he had even come to understand that although a person can improve and even prolong his life through the practice of "nurturing life," "mutually interacting" (*xiang-can*) with his environment in a beneficial manner, he still must give up that one overweening desire (*tan*) for physical immortality (*xian*-ship) and resign himself to following "nature's design" (*tian-ming*, a term suitably ambiguous to be translated as the "fate or lifespan Heaven has prepared for one," as long as we understand, as the Daoists did, that Heaven is not a supernatural agency but rather nature or life itself).

Like all of the other poems in this chapter, this poem is a record of one stage of an ongoing spiritual quest that ended only when Lu's life ended. When this poem was written he felt himself to have achieved a level of spiritual "transcendence" (*chao-ran*) due to the "broad awareness" (*shu-huo,* a term coined by Lu himself) that his many years of study and experience had brought him.

# CHAPTER 5

# In Vino Veritas:
## Poems After Drinking Wine

"WRITTEN While Drunk in the River Pavilion," a seven character Regulated Verse poem, was written when he was fifty-two and living in Chengdu.[1]

> Soaked and sotted with a hundred cups
>     I revel in River Pavilion;
> Carrying a candle, brandishing a brush,
>     my spirit still strong.
> In Heaven, so I've heard, stars serve the wine;
> 4  Among men we'd rather have ground to bury sorrow.
> In life I hope to be Li Guang called
>     Flying General;
>  In death I'll envy Liu Ling honored as
>     Drunken Marquis.
> Playfully entreat this beautiful one, "give us a smile"—
> 8  My sojourn in Brocade City's already reached six years!

Poems concerning the virtues of drinking wine (*yin-jiu*, primarily rice wine, often brewed at home, and taken warm in cups or bowls) and drunkenness (*zui*) have always been part of the stock repertoire of Chinese poets. For Lu You, however, drinking wine was an integral part of his daily lifestyle, and he wrote a very large number of poems after drinking wine. There are more than four hundred and fifty titles that contain the words wine (*jiu*), drunk (*zui*), or drinking (*yin* or *zhuo*). On nearly every page of his collection, regardless of the subject matter of the poems in question, we find him drinking while he is doing or discussing whatever he is writing about. He drank when he was sad or happy, when extremely busy with official work, or when at leisure. He drank alone late at night and

101

early in the morning before breakfast. Of course he drank when he was in the army, hunting, gambling, listening to singing girls, or entertaining courtesans; but he drank even more often after he was retired and living peacefully at home, especially when he went to the various local festivals to drink and dance with the villagers and peasants. From reading his verse it is hard to imagine an activity or a time during which he would not be drinking wine.

The above poem illustrates several aspects of his relationship with the fruit of fermentation. The first line contains the usual exaggerated account of the amount he could consume, "a hundred cups" (*bai-ke*) being a conservative figure. When he drank he got very drunk, and quite often described himself with an appropriate image derived from the flowing or dripping of water, which I have translated "soaked and sotted" (*lin-li*). Sometimes he used the term "rotten drunk" (*lan-zui*). His was no mere "poetic rapture" with wine. It sometimes elated him and made him "high," but it also made him quite drunk. It also made him feel that his "spirit's still strong" (*qi shang qiu*), and there is little he could not accomplish in his state of temporary euphoria. Thus he "carries a candle" (*bing-zhu*) to extend the days and "seize every joy" as Li Bo, Tao Yuan-ming, and the Han poets before them had advised. Many of his drinking poems express this *carpe diem* theme. More importantly, drunkenness helped him to "bury sorrow" (*mai-you*), to forget the sadness (usually *chou*) of his personal frustration and lack of accomplishments, of the nation's shame, and, much deeper still, of his own mortality.

The Flying General Li Guang, as we have seen, is often mentioned in his patriotic works. In his drinking poems he naturally alludes to other models. Liu Ling of the Jin dynasty, posthumously styled the Drunken Marquis (*zui-hou*), was a short, ugly, profligate, and self-indulgent eccentric of the "pure talk" (*qing-tan*) school. He was one of the famous Seven Sages of the Bamboo Grove, that included also Ruan Ji (210–63) and Xi Kang. He often rode around in a little cart pulled by a deer, carrying a jug of wine. He instructed his servants travelling with him to carry hoes and follow behind the cart. He told them to bury him without ceremony wherever they happened to be when he died. His best known exploit was tricking his wife, who disapproved of his constant drunkenness, into setting out a sacrifice of meat and wine to the gods before whom Liu promised to vow never to drink again. When his wife left he knelt down and prayed,

> Heaven has given birth to me, Liu Ling
> Who has acquired fame in drinking
> A gallon at one sitting,
> And half of that again to sober up.
> As for the wife's words
> It is best we don't listen!

Then he drank the wine and ate the meat and became quite drunk.[2] This allusion to Liu Ling introduces another major theme in Lu's drinking poems—that wine sometimes led him to feelings of great elation and transcendence similar to those he felt during meditation, that there was, indeed, "a taste of profundity"[3] for him in wine.

This poem was written after he had been living in the Chengdu area for nearly six years, and his own note to lines seven and eight says, "Han Yu wrote, 'The women of Yue smile once [and you] stay three years.'" Lu was, of course, upstairs in a wine shop drinking with a singing girl or courtesan as he so often did in Chengdu.

Many poems and lines from poems throughout his collection speak of his love of wine. "Facing the Wine," a five character Ancient Verse poem written at the age of fifty-six, is a good example.[4]

> Doctors beginning with He and Bian
> Have not written an age-banishing formula.
> But I've found it in my later years—
> 4 Nothing compares with fine barmy brew!
> One cup brings spring to your face;
> Think what several bowls will do.
> Sit and let peach blossoms redden,
> 8 Completely replace frosty yellow leaves.
> Looking in the mirror I want to dance for joy,
> Relive once again my youthful abandon!

Wine is depicted here as the elixir that can rejuvenate both man and nature. He and Bian were two early doctors from the ancient state of Qin. "Barmy brew" (*qu-nie*) is literally "yeast / barm and fermenting grain," and, along with "Master Yeast" (*qu-sheng*, "born of yeast"), is Lu's most commonly used metonymy for wine. The Chinese still say that a man in his cups has the colors of spring (*chun-se*) in his face, and spring is also the season of youth as well as a euphemism for sexual activity; thus, the image here is one of rejuvenation. The poem was written in the winter, but Lu still imagines the peach blossoms coming forth and replacing the yellow leaves of winter. The peach blossoms reddening almost certainly refers to the red cheeks or coquettish blushing of singing girls or courtesans. The company of the ladies and the wine, then, make him look and feel so young that he wants to dance and relive his days of "youthful abandon" (*shao-nian kuang*); *kuang* refers to active sexual adventures and the sort of "reckless abandon" Lu was indulging in at the time this poem was written.

In these four lines written when he was sixty, the wine causes him to "run recklessly" (*die-dang*) in a burst of spontaneity.[5]

> Love of mountains enters bone marrow;
> Desire for wine invades vital regions.
> Running recklessly beyond wind and mist;
> Singing and shouting beside barmy brew!

"Invades vital regions" (*zai gao-huang*) is the standard medical term for an incurable disease.

A very common self-representation, this time from a poem written at age seventy, also may refer to Lu's amorous adventures and account for his frequently sleeping until very late in the morning, if not into the afternoon.[6]

> Pawning clothes to buy wine, who discusses price?
> Carrying candles to admire flowers until dawn's light.

In his comparative poverty, Lu often spent more for wine than he could afford, not to mention what some other sorts of entertainment might cost; and nearly every spring, as sure as he would write about spring rains, he would mention pawning his clothes to purchase wine.

After his retirement, Lu tried as far as possible to emulate Tao Yuan-ming. "Festival Drinking," a seven character Regulated Verse poem written at age eighty, contains references to Tao's famous twenty drinking poems. The occasion was Lu's participation in a spring festival in Shanyin at which drinking, dancing, and singing always played a major part.[7]

> Rise and fall in this world are but a turn of the wheel;
> Success and failure are always just a throw of the dice.
> When I see a great drunkard hailed a worthy minister,
> 4   I begin to believe the "always sober" *is* a petty knave.
> Rising to dance I'll surely enjoy graybeards' company;
> Returning at dusk I'll also have young people's help.
> These days don't lack masters of color and wash—
> 8   Who'll paint *Three Mountain Festival Drinking Scene?*

Lu's note after line four quotes lines three and four from Tao's "Drinking Poem No. 13," "One is always getting drunk alone/ One stays sober all the year around."[8] Tao was referring to the two sides of his own personality, of which he preferred the drunken. These lines in Lu's poem refer to his being hailed as a "worthy minister" by the villagers; and, thus, he concludes that it is surely best to remain drunk. The rest of the poem depicts him dancing with the other old men of the village and being helped home by the young people. His mood is one of humor and happiness, and he wishes someone would paint a picture to capture the joy of the festival.

"Writing of Joy when the Wine is Ripe," a seven character Regulated Verse poem written at the age of eighty-three, humorously expresses his love of home-brewed wine through the use of two "unpoetic" images of a "bound criminal" (*ji-qiu*) and a "terrible itch" (*ke-yang*), colloquial expressions that were much used in Sung dynasty verse.[9]

> In little trough on spring night pressing spring brew,
> Heaven gave me Tortoise Hall to reward my efforts.

Joyful as a bound criminal hearing of imminent release.
4   Happy as a terrible itch getting a good scratch!
Cup and dipper not yet set out, my heart's first drunk;
Looking askance at river and hills, my spirit's already high.
Long detesting smell of meat, hating to lower chopsticks,
8   My eyes light up at lakeside trapping a pair of crabs!

Hyperbole concerning the great amounts of wine he consumed
is another common feature that runs throughout his works. A
short chronological sequence will give the general feeling. At
age forty-nine:[10]

In youthful abandon I played with wine, my spirit
        spitting rainbows;
One laugh not yet finished, thousand cups emptied!

At fifty:[11]

Wasting the day playing *Go* under sparse bamboos;
Sending off spring dead drunk among scattered flowers.

And:[12]

Draining cups as fast as Yellow River flows;
Brandishing brush sounding like white clouds scudding.

At fifty-nine:[13]

In youth I loved unrestrained heroics;
Seeing wine my spirit already downed it.
Once drinking I only counted the days—
No sense considering pints and buckets!

At seventy-three:[14]

The sky's cold, I want to get drunk with someone;
How can I change the Long River into muddy wine!

Finally, at seventy-seven:[15]

> Heaven and earth serve as my house;
> River and mountains are my guests.
> Using the North Dipper to pour wine,
> I regret my drinking capacity's slight!

These examples could, of course, be multiplied many times.

Thematically there are at least five distinct categories to be found among Lu's poems associated with drinking wine, and only three of them can rightly be classified as drinking poems. There are first of all poems written while drinking or written about drinking that express the common theme of seeking escape from sorrow in the "care dispelling thing" (*wang-you-wu*, Tao Yuan-ming's happy invention).[16] Then there are a number of poems, the finest ones in my estimation, in which drinking wine leads to true elation and euphoria. These poems actually seem to have been written under the influence of wine, or shortly after sobering up, and usually involve transcendent drunken journeys described in the diction of Daoism and the *Li Sao* tradition. Third, there are a great many short and humorous poems describing the aged poet falling down drunk on the roadside in his native Shanyin, being helped home by his son or other young people, dancing, singing, putting flowers in his hair, and generally acting in some eccentric fashion. The fourth category, which I will not deal with in this chapter, consists of a number of poems composed on the occasion of drinking wine that turn out to be patriotic laments in the heroic mode. The fifth residual category, as it were, consists of all those many occasional poems with wine (*jiu*) or drunk (*zui*) in the title that really have little or nothing to do with drinking or wine as such; they usually concern travel, hunting, local festivals, pastoral scenes, sending off friends, or other themes common to Chinese poetry.

In this chapter some representative examples of the first three major themes in Lu's drinking poems are presented. These themes also fall rather neatly into chronological order, in keeping with the general development of his poetry. The period of time spent in Chengdu and its environs during his late forties and early fifties was the most frustrating and depressing time in his entire life, and he sought solace in drinking and reckless living at that time. All of the best poems expressing the theme of "raising the cup to destroy sorrow" (*ju-bei xiao-chou*), in Li Bo's now proverbial phrase, come from that period. During that time he began to style himself the "Reckless Old Man" (*Fang-weng*), and he emerged from that period with a renewed interest in Daoism, alchemy, and even psychedelics, in which wine began to serve more as a source of high elation and transcendent euphoria than mere solace in sadness. From his middle fifties until his middle sixties, Lu wrote most of the finest of his drinking poems expressing true elation. His entire lifestyle became increasingly quietistic after the age of sixty-five, and especially in his seventies, and all of the best of the humorous, self-mocking, short poems on his drunken eccentricities were written after the age of sixty-five.

Lines nine to sixteen from a seven character Ancient Verse poem entitled "Written While Upstairs Drunk" demonstrate his conscious resort to feigned madness or eccentricity (*kuang*) in Chengdu in order to hide his shame and feelings of frustration. Of course, it is quite possible that despite his political complaints and frustrations he still enjoyed his misery to some extent and the chance for self-dramatization in verse.[17]

> In Yi-zhou's official tavern wine's like the sea;
> I come to untie their flag, negotiate their day's supply.
> Drunk with wine I play chess with happy abandon,
> 12  Or easily throw seven-eleven, shouting my joyous victory!
> On cow-back, dazzling brightly, lightning eyes glare—
> Madcap yes, but I tell you, not really mad.
> How dare this servant forget the ancient capital's
>       nine temples?
> 16  My ancestors' holy spirits are there beside the emperor's!

"Dazzling brightly, lightning eyes glare" (*lan-lan dian-mu guang*) is an allusion to Wang Rong of the Jin dynasty that Lu often used to describe himself when he was drunk. Wang was one of the Seven Sages of the Bamboo Grove. Highly precocious and eccentric, he was reputed to be able to look directly into the sun without blinking, and someone once said of him that his "eyes dazzled brightly like lightning under the cliffs" (*yan lan-lan ru yan-xia dian*).[18]

"Drinking Wine," a seven character Ancient Verse poem written at the age of forty-eight, argues rather humorously that wine is better than either Buddhism or Daoism in offering comfort in the face of sorrow and grief. Free will also plays a role in this philosophy of drinking, and the reader is left with his own choice of "dying in drunkenness or living in sadness" (*zui-si chou-sheng jun zi ze*).[19]

> Scholar Lu studying the Way lacks strength of will,
> His heaving breast cannot achieve peace and calm.
> Wryly laughs that hundred years have such grief and joy;
> 4  The myriad affairs should be exchanged for drunken delight.
> Sometimes many cares pile up, rising mountain high;
> I shout loudly, demanding wine to wash them all level.
> Are there not Daoist Masters and aged Chan monks in the world?
> 8  They can't compete with closing the door to commune with
> Master Yeast!
> Colleagues and friends for several years scattered like water;
> I have only warmer and dipper to share life and death.
> One day without seeing *them* makes one sad.
> 12  Day and night we share together without complaint.
> People say there's poison in barmy brew
> That rots ribs, pierces guts, hardens blood and veins.
> What pleases you in life, that you should do—
> 16  To die in drunkenness or live in sadness, you yourself
> must choose;

The final poem illustrating this theme is an Ancient Verse poem containing both five character and seven character lines. "Facing the Wine" was written at the age of fifty-one in Chengdu. It had been fourteen years since Lu had been an official in Hangzhou (symbolized by Changan in the poem) and he was feeling old and frustrated when he wrote this poem. Only wine and the company of young ladies ("beautiful flowers," "oriole," and "willow") can melt away his sorrows, and the "rosy cheeks" of his companions are worth more to him than the fancy dress uniforms that signify high office.[20]

> Restless sorrow like flying snow
> Entering wine instantly melts away.
> Beautiful flowers like old friends;
> 4  With one smile cups empty themselves.

Fluttering oriole has feelings to remember me—
At willow's edge all day sings in spring breeze.
Not visiting Changan full these fourteen years,
8    The drunkard always becomes a decrepit old man.
Nine fold jewelled sash, bright and gaily shining,
Cannot compare with keeping your two cheeks rosy.

"Drunken Song," a five character Ancient Verse poem written at the age of forty-eight, is selected to describe the feeling of high elation brought about by wine. Lu uses symbolic language to depict the elation of an imaginary underwater journey to the "Water Crystal Palace" (*shui-jing-gong*) of the dragon kings and the expansive feeling in which he imagines he can encompass rivers and mountains in his breast and spit forth rainbows with his breath.[21]

I drink in the River Pavilion,
With railing open on four sides.
Hand holding a white jade boat,
4    Body roams the Water Crystal Palace.
When once I sip the wine,
Rivers and hills fill my chest.
My heart engenders high elation,
8    Could spit forth a long rainbow!
About to spit, suddenly swallow back—
Greatly fear I'll startle the children!
In Heaven and Earth as vast as this,
12    There's no place for this old man.
When shall I call up a blue phoenix,
And ride away on million mile winds!

A "white jade boat" (*bai-yu-chuan*) is, of course, a kind of decorative wine cup. A "blue phoenix" (*qing-luan*), often mentioned in Lu's Daoist poems, would be the preferred mount of an immortal transcendent (*xian*).

"Drunken Song by the Side of a Pond," a seven character Ancient Verse poem written in his forty-eighth year, is one of the finest examples of Lu's poetry of drunken elation. Employing a hyperbolic diction reminiscent of the *Li Sao*, the one book he most liked to read when drinking heavily, and allusions to Li Bo, Daoist adepts, and sacred isles, he describes a euphoric vision of what he would do if he were an immortal: arrest the passage of time itself. The poem comes down to earth in the last four lines to end on the familiar note that, since immortality is forever beyond our reach, the next best thing is to get drunk and enjoy the elation that wine brings while forgetting the future and the transitory nature of human life. Lu was also once again enjoying the company of a courtesan (*ji*), presumably in a Chengdu wine shop.[22]

I want to erect a Transformed Immortal's Mid-Heaven tower,
Look down on the four seas—all flying dust.
Also want to build a Formulist Adept's seaworthy craft,
4   Break waves a myriad miles seeking the Mystic Isles.
Seize the sun and hang it on Magic Mulberry's branches;
Prolong the spring by pulling back North Dipper's handles.
With three foot horizontal flute make dragons sing,
8   While hundred-faced waist drums rival thunder's clap.
Drinking like a mighty whale drying up the seas,
Jade Mountain does not fall from high, lofty elation.
Half drunkenly remove my cap, hair's still black;
12   Strong heart quite unwilling to yield to downcast sorrow.
This morning my courtesan's like moon and flowers;
But dead men's white bones gather green moss.
The future will view today as today views the past—
16   Why should one refuse to get drunk on this fine wine?!

The first six lines relate the poet's desires to transcend this world. The *Lie Zi* tells of the "Transformed Immortals" (*hua-ren*) who told King Mu of the Zhou dynasty of their many exploits. The "Mid-Heaven tower" (*zhong-tian-zhi-tai*) may be an invention of Lu's own imagination, but H. P. Yoke comments that it reminds one of the "Eight Winds Tower" (*ba-feng-tai*) that the usurper Wang Mang built in 10 A.D. Wang hoped to become an immortal by offering sacrifices to the spirits on that tower.[23] A "Formulist Adept" (*fang-shi*), or "gentleman of the formula," is an alchemical magician or Daoist immortal who was supposed to know the secret "formula" (*fang*) for the elixir of immortality. Many of these men were active at Chinese courts throughout history, especially during the Han and Tang dynasties, when many emperors wished to sample their wares in hopes of achieving immortality, and not a few died of elixir poisoning. The "Mystic Isles" are Peng-lai, in this poem, Fang-zhang and Ying-zhou; they had been sought by Daoist-influenced explorers since the time of the first emperor of the Qin dynasty. He reportedly sent out the first expedition seeking these "Isles of the Blessed," but it never returned. Some say they actually landed in Japan.[24]

The next four lines relate what supernatural powers the poet will possess and what he will do with them after he reaches the "Mystic Isles" and becomes a "Transformed Immortal" himself. He would arrest the passage of time by hanging the sun back on the branches of the "Magic Mulberry" (*fu-sang*), actually a pair of legendary mulberry trees in the far east from which the sun was believed to rise every morning.[25] Then he would "pull back" (*wan-hui*) the handle of the "North Dipper" (*bei-dou*) in order to prevent it from ever swinging around as it would appear to do when the seasons changed from spring to autumn. The Chinese word for "sun" (*ri*) also means "day," and the word for "spring" (*chun*) also stands for one's youth, just as "autumn" (*qiu*) stands for the later years. Thus, these two feats of cosmic power would also be the very way in which the transformed one would preserve his immortality. These images are rather common in Chinese poetry, but the way in which Lu has employed them here is quite original. Next, he would play such music as would harmonize with the cosmos, making "dragons sing" (*long-yin*), an allusion to a poem by Li Bo, and "rivalling thunder's clap" (*sheng zhuan-lei*).

His cosmic powers would be topped off by a feat of super-human drinking. "Jade Mountain" (*yu-shan*) was a common epithet for handsomeness of appearance, but "jade mountain collapsing/ falling down" (*beng* or *dao*) is a description of a person's drunken appearance that first occurs in the *Shi-shuo xin-yu* collection of anecdotes about eccentrics of the North-South dynasties period, such as the Seven Sages of the Bamboo Grove. Two lines from Li Bo's poem "Song of Xiang-yang" (*xiang-yang ge*) are, "Do not need one cash to buy clear wind and bright moon, / Jade mountain falls by itself with no one pushing" (*qing-feng ming-yue bu-yong yi-qian mai, yu-shan zi-dao fei ren tui*). Lu is thus implying here that he is an even more accomplished drinker than the legendary Li Bo. "High lofty elation" (*gao cui-wei*), usually used to describe mountains, is the term that Lu commonly uses in referring to his drinking "high."

The last six lines of the poem return to the poet's actual situation. In a characteristic gesture, modelled no doubt on Tao Yuan-ming, he takes off his official cap and notes that his hair is still black—that he is still young. He then vows that his "strong heart" (*zhuang-xin*) will not give in to the sadness deriving from his frustrated hopes for a northern expedition. He would rather transcend his frustration in drunkenness and forget his troubles in the company of beautiful courtesans. The last two lines, an excellent motto for advocates of the *carpe diem* philosophy, are very nearly literary prose, a good example of the well-known "prosization" (*san-wen-hua*) of Sung poetry. The addition of only one character, understood when read as poetry, would make these lines prose: *hou dang shi jin ru [jin] shi gu, dui jiu xi zui he wei zai*, literally: "The future will view today as [today] views the past,/ with (facing) wine begrudge drunkenness, how/ why act (thus)!"

"Song of a Drunken Fall," a seven character Ancient Verse poem written when he was sixty-seven, though still expressing the theme of drunken transcendence, is also very close to the last category of humorous poems.[26]

> In times past when facing wine I dared not drink;
> Glancing around, all sides held snares and traps.
> Wanted to speak wild words, feared guests would talk;
> 4  Unable to smile completely, worried troubles grew.
> But today, falling down drunk by official roadside
> With flowers in hair, fear not wildest eccentricities!
> Passers-by's shouts arouse me, all the more elated;
> 8  Young cowherd helps me home, still stagger and stumble.
> I begin to realize man finds his own pleasure in life;
> A foolish plan to take office, always tremble in fear.
> An autumn hair's gain or loss is not worth discussing;
> 12  Ten thousand age's rise and fall—one drunken pillow!

"A foolish plan" (*wu-ji*) is probably a reference to Tao Yuan-ming's "Drinking Poem No. 10," "Since this [taking office]

was not a famous plan (*ming-ji*) / I stopped my cart and came
back home."²⁷ An "autumn hair" (*qiu-hao*) is considered to be
the smallest thing in the world and here expresses extreme be-
littlement of the world, past and present.

"Drunken Song," a seven character Ancient Verse poem
written when the poet was nearly sixty-nine, demonstrates his
continuing flare for self-dramatization and his resolve to model
himself on the Seven Sages of the Bamboo Grove, getting drunk
until dawn, singing, and dancing to his heart's content, completely contemptuous of the simpering courtiers of the capital.²⁸

> Of thirty-six strategies, drunkenness is especially wondrous;
> The several gentlemen of Bamboo Grove are truly my mentors.
> *Xiao, xiao,* the autumn wind blows my sidelocks.
> 4   Crab claws are easily picked up with the left hand.
> Fallen down drunk on village road, my son helped me home;
> Staring at him without recognition, I asked who he was.
> Loudly singing, rose to dance, the night being young;
> 8   North Dipper shone clearly as Bright River flowed on.
> Noble ones refusing drunkenness made themselves foolish;
> Bridling horses with yellow gold to impress market children.
> One morning when calamity came, none stood firm;
> 12   *Xin-zhou,* like a mountain, could not be moved.

Line one changes the original proverb, "Of the thirty-six
strategies, running away is the best." In line four, presumably the
left hand is used to pick up crab claws because his right hand
is occupied holding the wine cup. The "Bright River" (*ming-he*)
in line eight is, of course, the Milky Way, as well as an image
for the amount of wine he consumes. The allusion contained
in the last four lines is unclear, but the "noble ones" (*gui-ren*),
a term of opprobrium with Lu, seems to refer to the courtiers
of the late Han and North-South dynasties periods who refused
to employ the strategy of drunkenness used by the Seven Sages
of the Bamboo Grove, especially Ruan Ji, as a form of pro-
tective cover to avoid political involvement during a very
dangerous period. The "calamity" (*huo*) mentioned in line
eleven would, by this reading, refer to the collapse of whichever
state they happened to be serving in order that they might dress

so regally in front of the common people in the markets. The last line, however, remains unexplained.

Finally, in "Sighing Without Wine," a five character and seven character Ancient Verse poem written at the age of seventy-four, Lu's sense of humor shows again as he jokes with the "Creator of Things" (*zao-wu*), nature itself, whom he blames for the "cruel trick" (*nüe-xi*) of making it difficult for him to obtain wine. He laughs it off by implying that he is perfectly capable of practicing "sober madness" (*xing-kuang*)—being just as eccentric as ever even without the aid of wine.[29] The first two sets of four lines each are parallel stanzas that employ a free and proselike diction, beginning with the words *bu-yong*, "[I] don't need," or "[there's] no need [to . . .]."

> Don't need to dam the Yellow River.
> Don't need to dig up Zhou tripods.
> I only want a house full of wine,
> 4 Day and night drunk without waking!
> Don't need a cap like a winnowing fan.
> Don't need a seal like a bushel basket.
> I only want a body strong and healthy,
> 8 Morning and evening ever drinking wine!
> Creator of Things shows little mercy;
> His cruel tricks every day renewed.
> Sits and lets my old copper bowl
> 12 Gather dust these many months.
> All my life obtaining wine I was wild beyond compare;
> Hundred scrolls gushed and flowed: driving wind and rain!
> Creator of Things now wants to weary me with sobriety—
> 16 But you've never known this old one's sober madness!

CHAPTER 6

# The Illuminated Commonplace:
# Poems in Response to Nature

LIVING in an unpolluted, nonindustrial age, and travelling far and wide over so much of the Chinese landscape, Lu You was always surrounded by the beauty and awesomeness of natural forces. He enjoyed them, he marvelled at them, and he often wrote of them in his poetry. Although he can not rightly be called a "landscape poet," nevertheless he had a very deep love for the natural world. He shared the philosophy of the great Sung landscape painters, deriving ultimately from Daoism and Chan Buddhism, that mankind is an integral part of nature and that man's place is *in nature* not outside of it or above it. His expressed response to nature was sometimes one of sadness that man's life, rooted in everyday time, seems to be over so quickly, while nature seems to renew itself yearly and partake of universal time. This was perhaps the most common response to nature in Chinese poetry before the Sung dynasty. More often, however, he expressed an expansive feeling of freedom, spontaneity, and joy in the presence of natural phenomena.

Critics distinguish two broadly defined types of "nature poetry" in Chinese: the "landscape" or *shan-shui*, "mountain and water"; and the "pastoral" or *tian-yuan*, "field and garden." The first generally describes the more powerful and awesome aspects of nature, such as high mountains, great waterfalls, or mighty tempests. The second characteristically depicts the quieter aspects of nature, such as a gentle spring rainfall, scenes of planting and reaping, the blooming of flowers, and the flight of butterflies. Xie Ling-yun and Tao Yuan-ming are the acknowledged masters of the two styles respectively.

During Lu's very long poetic career, his interest in nature and his production of poetry in response to nature evolved quite

116

naturally from an early emphasis on landscape to a later pre-occupation with the pastoral. His landscape poems, written during his many travels before the age of sixty-four, may be divided thematically into three basic types: travel poems per se, depicting some natural scene and his response to it; poems expressing a Daoistic philosophy of freedom and joy; and "true landscapes" in the sense that they portray a particular scene in an almost painterly manner with great attention to detail and only slight reference to human response. His pastoral poems, written with ever-increasing frequency after his retirement at the age of sixty-four, may also be divided into four general types: poems presenting an idealized picture of rural life, the way he *felt* it to be; poems expressing his love of his home in Shanyin; poems describing the customs and the people of Shanyin, often used as a vehicle to speak for the peasants; and poems expressing social concern for the lives of the peasants and criticism of the Sung government. The poems in this chapter constitute a representative selection of these various types and include those works most often found in modern anthologies.

## I  *Landscape Poems*

"Traveling the Qu-Tang Gorge," a seven character Ancient Verse poem, was written at the age of forty-five just before or just after arriving in Kui-zhou in Sichuan early in the winter of 1170.[1]

    Fourth month nearly over, fifth month coming on,
    How majestic the swelling waters of the gorge:
    Wave flowers floated aloft: snow on a hot road.
4  Rapid stones rolled angrily: thunder on a clear day.
    A thousand boats and ten thousand barks dared not cross;
    Polemen and ruddermasters' courageous hearts shattered.
    Every man waited with folded arms for the force to abate;
8  Who dared lightly set forth and risk strange calamity?
    One morning the season past, waters couldn't hold it;
    Mountainside only retained a scar traced in the sand.
    You did not see:
    Master Lu at year's end arriving in Kui-zhou,
12  Qu-Tang Gorge waters as smooth as oil!

The first eight lines imaginatively describe the force of the rapids in a midsummer flood, a scene that Lu did not witness at that time. The next two lines depict the scene at the gorge when Lu actually passed through it and demonstrate his close observation of nature—only a "scar traced in the sand" (*sha-hen*) halfway up the cliff marks the water's midsummer height. The sight of that scar probably gave him the idea to write the poem. The last two lines, introduced by the conventional *yue-fu* phrase, *jun bu-jian*, announces Lu's rather triumphant arrival in Kui-zhou after a five month journey.

"Travelling by Boat between Pure Penny and Axe-Handle Bridge," written at the age of seventy-seven on the way home from a year of editorial work in Hangzhou, is a fine example of Lu's seven character Regulated Verse.[2]

> Over a year dream-longing for Kuai-ji City;
> Joyfully hang high sails, go freely flowing.
> Before spying east and west paired white pagodas,
> 4  We'll first pass north and south twin Pure Pennies.
> Young boys fingering flutes welcome returning argosies;
> Old men with jugs and cups express parting sentiments.
> Thinking that at my home night has not yet fallen,
> 8  Between bamboos I just glimpse the setting sun's glow.

The first couplet introduces the problem: his longing for home while in Hangzhou. The next two couplets elaborate on the theme of going home. He thinks ahead to the two white pagodas that stood outside Kuai-ji and Shanyin on the river, but he must first pass "twin Pure Pennies" (*liang qian-qing*), two areas along the river so named because of a story about an incorruptible (*qing*, "pure, clean") official who threw a bribe (*qian*, "cash") into the water there. Lu witnesses other people's reunions and partings as the boat moves along the river ever nearer to his home. The final couplet suggests the resolution of the problem in his imminent arrival home. As with Su Dong-po's poem mentioned by Yoshikawa, and in contrast to Tang dynasty poetry, the "setting sun" (*xi-yang*) gives him a feeling of peace rather than sadness.[3]

"Strange Stones by My Jian-yang Studio," the first poem I've selected to express the Daoist philosophy of transcendence, is a seven character Ancient Verse poem written when he was forty-seven.[4] It may be properly introduced by a quotation from the autobiography of the late C. G. Jung:[5]

It was strangely reassuring and calming to sit on my stone. Somehow it would free me of all my doubts. Whenever I thought that I was the stone, the conflict ceased. "The stone has no uncertainties, no urge to communicate, and it is eternally the same for thousands of years." I would think, "while I am only a passing phenomenon which bursts into all kinds of emotions, like a flame that flares up quickly and then goes out." I was but the sum of my emotions, and the Other in me was the timeless, imperishable stone.

The full title tells a story:

There are many strange stones by my office in Jia-yang (Jia-zhou), scattered and abandoned with no one to understand them. I began to collect them to make an artificial mountain and thus renamed my West Studio the Little Mountain Hall. I wrote this short song for the occasion.

Of ancient men what man so loved cliffs and valleys,
These hills being incomplete, collected curious stones?
Scattered and fallen they can prop beds or weight wine crocks;
4  Some large to fill a cart, some small to cover with the fist.
Secluded one making chance encounter heaves a happy sigh,
Long well rope quickly draws cold spring washing water.
Lofty peaks and deep ravines alternately erupting and swallowing;
8  Azure ranges and vermilion cliffs distantly meet and intertwine.
Stones cannot speak,, their meaning can be known—
Ask me why I feel sorrow in my lonely isolation.
"Human world's flourish and decay naturally have their seasons;
12  Abandoned *then,* why so hurt, *today,* why so happy?"
This saying is truly wondrous, but I'm so unworthy;
How dare refuse a forfeit drink before stony friends?
"For you I'll gladly make a ten day sojourn—
16  In my eyes the same as true mountain climbing!"

The message of the stones is essentially the same lesson that Zhuang Zi tried to teach to his pedantic friend Hui Zi: do not let your feelings of joy *or* sorrow harm your basic nature. The following dialogue is from the *Zhuang Zi*, Chapter Five.[6]

Hui Zi said to Zhuang Zi, "Can a man really be without feelings?"
Zhuang Zi: "Yes."
Hui Zi: "But a man who has no feelings—how can you call him a man?"
Zhuang Zi: "The Way gave him a face; Heaven gave him a form—why can't you call him a man?"
Hui Zi: "But if you've already called him a man, how can he be without feelings?"
Zhuang Zi: "That's not what I mean by feelings. When I talk about having no feelings, I mean that a man doesn't allow likes or dislikes to get in and do him harm. He just lets things be the way they are and doesn't try to help life along."

"Climbing East Mountain," a seven character Regulated Verse poem written in his seventieth year, expresses Lu's common feeling of joy in nature and resistance in adversity.[7]

Lacquer Garden proud officer's "Secret of Nurturing Life,"
Millet Hamlet lofty sage's "Return Home Now"—
Reckless Old Man's best-received new lessons:
4  Why not transcend the dusty world here and now!
Pine-bordered cliff rises, nearing Woodcutter Village;
Bamboo path, snakily winding, ascending Singing Tower.
Seeing off the setting sun, hills grow *more* beautiful.
8  Treading the moon with you, return loudly singing!

The first two couplets recall the lessons he's learned from Zhuang Zhou, the "Lacquer Garden Officer" (*qi-yuan li*), and Tao Yuan-ming, who once lived in "Millet Hamlet" (*su-li*). He had probably been rereading "The Secret of Nurturing Life," Chapter Three of the *Zhuang Zi*, and "Return Home Now," or simply "The Return," Tao Yuan-ming's famous apology for leaving office and returning to his rural home. Both Zhuang Zhou and Tao, in Lu's view, "transcended the dusty world" (*tuo chen-ai*) of cares and troubles while ostensibly still dwelling in it, just as he was doing in his retirement and in his ascent of this mountain—his journey into nature's scenic beauty.

The third couplet describes the mountain scene through the use of two literary allusions. The place name "Woodcutter Village" (*qiao-wu*) is mentioned in Tao Yuan-ming's "Peach

Blossom Spring," and thus associates East Mountain with that Shangri-la where time stood still. The "Singing Tower" (*xiao-tai*), an allusion to the *Book of Songs* poem "The River Has Branches" (*jiang you si*), refers to the mountain as a place of joy and freedom where one might spontaneously shout or sing.[8]

In the last couplet Lu characteristically reverses the meaning of a well-known Tang dynasty image, demonstrating, as he did in his "Plum Blossom Quatrain No. 3," cited by Yoshikawa, a typically Sung spirit of resistance and the feeling that life is of long duration.[9] Lines three and four of Li Shang-yin's "Le-you Heights," in James J. Y. Liu's translation, are: "The setting sun has infinite beauty— / Only, the time is approaching nightfall!" (*xi-yang wu-xian hao, zhi-shi jin huang-hun*).[10] Lu's line is literally: "Seeing off the setting sun to exhaustion, the hills are all the more beautiful" (*song-jin xi-yang shan geng-hao*). The contrast with the melancholy sentiments of the Tang poet is obvious and deliberate. Thus, he returns home "loudly singing" (*hao-ge*) for joy.

The final philosophical landscape poem to be examined again expresses a feeling of profound freedom and spontaneity in nature. "Leisurely Walking Among the Villages in Early Summer" is a seven character Regulated Verse poem written at the age of seventy-nine.[11]

> Thin clouds hiding the sun, day cannot brighten;
> Wild waters entering the lake gradually grow calm
> Verdant leaves suddenly lower, know a bird's landing.
> 4  Green duckweeds slightly move, sense fish swimming.
> Drunkenly roaming in complete abandon not knowing
>     where I'm going.
> Rising from slumber to freedom and ecstasy that's
>     not easily told.
> Suddenly encounter the secluded gentlemen of the lakeside—
> 8  Clasp hands and laugh together enjoying our abundant lives!

This poem is also characteristic of the regulated poem in that the first half describes the natural scene (*jing*) and the second half depicts human actions and feelings (*qing*). The second couplet is an especially fine example of Lu's close observation of nature, and we can easily believe that he really saw what he describes. The third couplet has an unmistakable Daoist flavor with its "drunken roaming" (*zui-you*), "complete abandon" (*fang-dang*), and "freedom and ecstasy" (*xiao-yao*). *Xiao-yao-you*, "Free and Easy Wandering," is the title of the first chapter of the *Zhuang Zi*, and carries the theme of "roaming" in nature further, to include the transcendence of the everyday world and the human consciousness, and the liberation of the true self in a feeling of unity with the cosmos. Lu often wrote of the "secluded gentleman of the lakeside" (*hu-bian yin-jun-zi*), so much so that his friend Yang Wan-li wrote that he meant himself. Perhaps it would be too much to say that the final couplet implies that he found his real self in nature and felt great joy and comfort (*wei*, my "enjoying") in his "abundant life" (*yu-sheng*), years lived beyond the normal span alloted to man.

The next two poems seem to me to be true landscapes. "Happiness Studio," a seven character Ancient Verse poem written when he was forty-eight, describes in great detail a very small tableau—the little studio by the East Lake in Shuzhou, Sichuan—the cool pavilion, completely isolated, quiet (*jing*), and leisurely (*xian*)—and is quite remarkable for its consistent use of parallelism in the Ancient Verse form.[12]

> East Lake in midsummer, wild grasses and trees,
> An old room without guests, cool noontime pavilion.
> Day lilies barely burgeoning do not see the sun;
> 4  Bamboo shoots peel themselves, blowing sweet a while.
> Wild ivy twisting and turning enters window cracks;
> Moist mildew in great profusion grows on roof beams.
> Straddling the ditch a few branches, most secretly secluded;
> 8  Swelling waters reached the threshold, rain ruined the walls.
> Quietly soaking, green duckweeds dance with water grasses;
> Leisurely roosting, white egrets swim with mandarin ducks.
> Lotus petals quite fragile though still thick and lush;
> 12  Blinding eyes, turquoise cloak conceals rouge complexion.
> Ought to roll up water-wrinkled precious mat;
> Too listless to unfold moon-round white fan.
> Heaven wind suddenly sends pagoda bell's voice,
> 16  Wakes me from pure reverie roaming Xiao and Xiang!

Line twelve refers to the leaves of the lotus flowers that re-
flect the sun's brightness, "blind the eyes" (*zhao-yan*), and cover
the "rouge complexion" (*hong-zhuang*) of the lotus petals like a
"turquoise cloak" (*cui-gai*); all of these are, of course, images
of feminine beauty. In the last line Lu pays a very great compli-
ment to the beauty of the East Lake area by comparing it to the
scenic Xiao-Xiang region in Hunan made famous in Chinese
landscape painting first by Sung Di's *Eight Scenes of Xiao and
Xiang* (*xiao-xiang ba-jing*).

"Drunkenly Descending Qu-Tang Gorge, in Midstream Watch-
ing the Stone Cliff's Flying Waters" is a seven character Ancient
Verse poem written during the poet's fifty-second year, while
descending the Yangzi River on the way home from Sichuan. It
is both a travel and a landscape poem in that it combines an
imaginative and detailed description of a waterfall with the
depiction of human actions and feelings in the presence of such
a natural wonder.[13]

> My thirty foot boat like a great green dragon
> Rides wind in soaring dance descending from Heaven.
> River flow strikes the earth: white brine billows!
> 4  Stone Beauty rides the waves: just like a horse!
> Boatmaster drinks heavily from white jade cup;
> Under sail, painted drums beat like spring thunder.
> Looking back, already lost West Nang Market.
> How wondrous:
> 8  A thousand yard sheer sloping green cliff.
> Green cliff, center split, where silver river flies,
> A million chests of fine pearls careen through space!
> Drunken face simply must welcome wild drops—
> 12  Capital's dust will not soil *my* travelling clothes!

The first four lines concentrate on the scene. An awesome
other-worldly mood is created with the image of the boat dancing like a dragon as it descends from Heaven. The white water
in the rapids (this time Lu was there during the period of high
water) crashes on the rocks and looks like brine in a salt field.
"Stone Beauty" is my own translation for the famous *Yan-yu*
rock formation that stood in the river at this point. When the
water was at its midsummer height, the boatmen had a saying:

"Yan-yu big as a horse, Qu-Tang cannot be descended." The next two lines describe the actions of the people on board his boat. Of course, he is the "boatmaster" (*zhu-ren*) who is imbibing heavily. The boatmen traditionally beat drums when they set out into the current after a rest. Lines seven to ten again return to the scene, first emphasizing the speed at which they are travelling and then describing the waterfall tumbling down the cliffside into the gorge below. A "silver river" (*yin-he*), also a conventional terms for the Milky Way, flies down the side of the cliff, the fine drops of the falls seeming like "fine pearls" (*zhu-ji*) careening through space. The last two lines describe the poet's reaction to this scene. He bares his drunken face to the falling water as if to wash his travelling clothes and vows that the "capital's dust" (*jing-chen*) will not soil them—he will remember his feelings at this moment and will not be corrupted by city life again.

## II  *Pastoral Poems*

The first of our pastoral poems, "Peasants of Yue Pool," a seven character Ancient Verse poem written at the age of forty-seven when Lu was travelling from Kui-zhou to Han-zhong in Sichuan on official business, expresses his idealized view of peasant life, or "peasant joys" (*nong-jia-le*) as he liked to call it.[14] Modern leftist critics are quite hard on him for expressing such views in light of the irrefutable evidence to the contrary. The life of the Chinese peasants was difficult during the best of times, and often it was miserably unbearable. As we shall see in this chapter, Lu was well aware of the many problems of the peasants, and he laid the blame for much of the peasants' misery at the door of the rich landlords and government officials. In office he attempted to lessen taxes, participated in disaster relief efforts, and applauded similar efforts by other good officials, such as his friend Zhu Xi (1130–1200). In this poem, however, it is the seasonal regularity, the quiet, and the harmony with Nature and man that he felt as he watched the peasants and other rural people that are uppermost in his mind. Just like city dwellers today who spend a couple of weeks on a farm or in the mountains trying to "get away from it all," Lu felt good in the company of peasants and farmers.

> Deep into spring peasant family's still busy plowing;
> In level fields shouts urge on teams of yellow oxen.
> Dirt dissolves leaving no clods, water begins to muddy;
> 4   Rainfall makes fine traces, sprouts now turn green.
> Time to transplant green sprouts, beautiful wind and sun.
> Their days are now peaceful with little corvee or taxes.
> Buying flowers at west house, joyfully make a marriage;
> 8   Carrying wine to east neighbors, celebate a son's birth.
> Who says peasant families are not thoroughly modern?
> Young girls paint themselves city style eyebrows!
> Many pairs of jade white arms, to all quite unknown!
> 12  Village empties, running and shouting, to watch them
>         pulling silk!
> Peasant families, peasant families, joy follows joy;
> Not like market and court's evil contention and strife.
> What have I really gained from my official travels?
> 16  For three years already I've neglected agriculture.

This poem, of course, expresses the common theme that rural life is far superior to the "contention and strife" (*zheng-duo*) of "market and court" (*shi-chao*) and that he was wasting his time in unrewarding official travels when he could be tilling the soil and living in peace and harmony at home.

After his retirement, Lu wrote many more poems expressing his feelings of freedom, joy, and love of his home in Shanyin; poems like the following two have been selected from many similar poems written over a span of more than twenty years. The first one, a seven character Regulated Verse poem, was written shortly after he returned to his home in 1189. The title again tells a story: "Reaching my Old Hills on the Tenth Day of the Seventh Month, I cut open a melon and brewed some tea, and suddenly felt very relaxed."[15]

> Mirror Lake's sheer beauty surpasses eastern pines;
> My house sits on lake mountain's number one peak.
> Cold melons: frosty knife splitting green jade.
> 4   Fragrant tea: copper mill breaking black dragons.
> Laugh that my strong heart, though old, still remains;
> Though well I know people cannot brook my wild ways.
> I'll beat a drum in a narrow lane and sing of "kingly might"—
> 8   What's to prevent me meeting in person Yao and Shun!

The first couplet merely sets the scene, while the second illuminates his commonplace everyday activities through the images of the melons like "green jade" (*bi-yu*) and tea like "black dragons" (*cang-long*). The third couplet expresses his lingering feelings of frustration that although he is still strong he is unwanted in official service because of his eccentricity (*kuang-tai*, "wild ways"). The final couplet presents his resolution to retire to a "narrow lane" (*qiong-yan*), play music, and sing a song of great peace that was sung by old men of eighty and ninety during the reign of the sage kings Yao and Shun. One version of this well-known folk song is as follows:[16]

> Sun comes up and we work,
> Sun goes down and we rest.
> Dig wells to drink,
> Till the soil to eat.
> What does the king's might have
>     to do with us!

The Chinese have a saying that describes the perfect harmony that should ideally exist between man and nature and in human society: "Heaven has its seasons, Earth has its benefits, and People have their agreeableness" (*tian-shi, di-li, ren-he*). "East and West Families," a five character Ancient Verse poem written when he was seventy-three, describes two families living in just such natural and close harmony. The effect in Chinese is quite remarkable and one can easily imagine why the poet wanted to live there with them.[17]

> From east family clouds clear the peaks,
> At west family cover half the mountain.
> West family's stream descends the valley,
> 4 At east family sounds like tinkling jade.
> Directly opposite, separated by narrow fences,
> Each possesses a three room thatched hut.
> With celery soup and wheaten gruel,
> 8 They visit back and forth each day.
> Sons and daughters like one family;
> Even dogs and chickens relax together.
> I too long to live nearby—
> 12 Please don't begrudge some surplus land!

The majority of Lu's pastoral poems and the most interesting to students of Chinese society and history are those that present vignettes of Shanyin life. "Song of Offering to the Gods," a seven character Ancient Verse poem with typical *yue-fu* style variations, was written when the poet was sixty-eight.[18] *Sai-shen*, also sometimes *sai-she*, means to make offerings or sacrifices to the gods in hopes of a plentiful year. In Sung times this festival was celebrated twice a year, in spring and autumn. Wine and food were offered to the gods of the fields, and the people drank wine, danced, sang, and generally enjoyed a pleasant holiday. Lu loved to attend these festivals to drink and dance with the local people.

Beat the drums—boom! boom!
Play the recorders—ta! ta!
An aged shaman stands forth robed in green with
    a staff of ash.
4   A young maiden dances around in red blouse and
    embroidered skirt.
Tallow candles shine brightly, brighter than wax.
Savory rich carp chowder comes from magic kitchens.
The aged shaman comes forward to pray,
8   As the young maid holds the wine jar:
"We want the gods to come and receive lasting
    joy and pleasure!
Let our fine grain be harvested by cartfuls,
Our cattle returning at dusk fill our barns,
12   Our chickens and ducks breed by the hundreds!
Grant us gain from harvest to harvest.
Remit all taxes from year to year.
Let rush whips not be used,
16   And prison yards stand empty!
Pleat straw to make officials who've only outward form.
Carve wood to fashion clerks with no official books.
Pure customs return again to Sage Emperor's days—
20   Cords not even knotted, using no "clever devices."
Gods returned, people scatter, drunkenly leaning together;
Deep in the night, singing and dancing by official roadside.

In writing a description of the rural festival rites and recounting the prayer of the old shaman, Lu has also offered a criticism of Sung officialdom and a plea for a return to the society of primitive communality. The "Sage Emperor" mentioned in line nineteen is Xi Huang, another name for the legendary Fu Xi, who was credited with the invention of writing and of the trigrams of the *Book of Changes*. In the Daoist description of primitive Chinese society, cords were said to have been knotted as a method of counting, but all other "clever devices" (not actually in the text) to make life more mechanical and society more easily controlled were to be eschewed.

The next series of four seven character quatrains, "Roaming to a Nearby Village in a Small Boat, I Left the Boat and Walked Back," were written at the age of seventy.[19] Du Fu popularized the practice of writing long series of quatrains on one theme, and Lu very often wrote series containing as many as twelve poems.

I

Several families' thatched huts make a village;
Gates closed in daytime, rice hulling sounds.
Cold sun about to sink, green mists rising—
Everywhere in the world are Peach Blossom Springs.

II

Borrowed a fishing boat to ascend this small stream;
Tied the boat at water's edge, returned on my staff.
Don't say rural villages are so sad and dreary—
Far surpass drowning dust of capital horses' hooves!

III

I do not even understand what is called sadness,
Leisurely roaming down east land and west walk.
Little boys all say, "the gentleman's drunk,
Snapping off yellow flowers to cover his head!"

IV

In slanting sun by ancient willows at Zhao Family Farm,
An old blind man carrying a drum just now begins his show.
Who cares about "right and wrong" after he's dead?
Whole village listens to the story of Master Cai.

The first poem here expresses the feeling that the Shanyin countryside is a "Peach Blossom Spring" (*tao* [*hua*] *yuan*), the Chinese Shangri-la from the poem by Tao Yuan-ming.[20] The second poem again expresses the theme that rural life is superior to urban living. The third poem mentions the autumn chrysanthemums, the "yellow flowers" (*huang-hua*), Tao Yuan-ming's favorites, and again demonstrates Lu's spontaneity and freedom in nature. The fourth poem depicts an entire village turning out at dusk to listen to a blind storyteller recount the tale of Cai Yong, or Cai Bo-jie, of the Later Han dynasty, and Zhao Wu-niang, the wife that he deserted when he became an official. Later in the Ming dynasty this story would be written up as a Southern Drama (*nan-xi*) by Gao Ming with the title of *Lute Song* (*Pi-pa Ji*) from the lute that Zhao Wu-niang carried when she went looking for her husband.[21]

The next three poems present local individuals that Lu often saw as he travelled around Shanyin. "A Young Cowherd," a five character Regulated Verse poem written in his seventy-fourth year, describes quite nicely one day in the life of the boy.[22] In the first couplet we see him taking the water buffalo out in the morning; there is a slight hint of danger, but the second couplet assures us that all is going to be well. The third couplet describes the day coming to an end with an afternoon rain and the smoke from cooking fires rising through the trees. Finally the boy comes home safe and sound, making his father feel quite relieved.

> Stream's deep, no need to worry,
> Wu buffalo can easily swim it.
> Young boy straddles buffalo's back,
> 4  Safe and steady as riding a boat.
> Cold rain, hillsides grow distant,
> Vague, blurred, smoky trees . . . dusk.
> Hearing a flute old man comes out to welcome—
> 8  The boy returned, the buffalo enters its pen.

"The Old Dame," written the next spring, is a self-explanatory seven character quatrain.[23]

> Going to festival south of town, hastily entering the lake,
> Old granny of antique countenance, seventy and still strong.
> Even carries her rusty, dusty marriage day mirror—
> Powdering here and rouging there, all to no avail.

"Presented to Old Wang the Firewood Seller while Boating on Jin's Family Channel" is the second of four seven character quatrains with the same title. It was written at the age of eighty-one, and one cannot help thinking that Lu saw himself in Old Wang.[24]

> Old man no longer labors at agricultural tasks;
> Still doesn't forget to count off chicks and pigs.
> Washing his feet, lying in bed, feels truly happy—
> Little grandson, gradually grown, can now cook soup!

The last poem in this chapter, written with extreme simplicity of diction, in keeping with the language of the peasants it speaks for, presents a moving picture of peasant life and feelings, as well as a strong criticism of the Sung government's treatment of these forgotten men upon whom their entire social system depended.[25] The peasants work hard at "the basic occupation" (*ben-ye*, "agriculture"), hoping only to enjoy peace and security. Instead, they are oppressed by tax collectors and dragged off to courts, where all law was penal law and one was assumed guilty until proven innocent, usually by bribing the jailor; there they are beaten without mercy. Finally, when they return home and want to tell everyone in the family of their wretched treatment, their tender feelings and respect for their aged parents prevents them from venting their anger. The title of this five character Ancient Verse poem is "Peasant Lament"; it was written in his sixty-ninth year.

> In the highlands we all plant wheat;
> In the waterlands we all plant rice.
> The ox's collar cuts him to the bone;
> 4  Shout him on! Still plowing at night.
> Toiling at agriculture with all our might,
> All we desire is to enjoy general peace.
> Who's that knocking before the gate?
> 8  County clerks come to collect taxes.
> Once we're dragged into the county courts,
> Day and night we're beaten without cease.
> What man is not afraid of dying?
> 12  We reckon we've no hope of living.

Returning home, wanting to tell all,
We fear to hurt our parents' feelings.
If the old ones get enough to eat,
16    Wives and children are feather-light burdens!

## CHAPTER 7

# The Liveliness of Dreams

CHAPTER one sketched the development of Lu You's personality in terms of the tension and interaction between two contrasting forces—the inner world of imagination and spiritual quest, and the outer world of social responsibility and service. As Lu grew older, especially after his retirement at sixty-four, his inner personality began to exert a greater and greater influence on his life and work. Nowhere perhaps is this inner personality and its development more apparent than in those poems whose titles state clearly that they were either composed while actually dreaming and written down from memory immediately upon waking or that they record things experienced in dreams.

The Qing Dynasty critic and admirer of Lu's poetry, Zhao Yi (1727–1814), was the first to comment on the great number of dream poems in his collection; but he believed that no one could have so many dreams and actually remember them. He thought that Lu first wrote the poems without title and then afterwards gave them a title that said they were records of dreams.[1] I believe that nothing could be further from the truth. Like Jung or Wordsworth or Goethe, Lu had what Wordsworth called "the power of a peculiar eye," a kind of eidetic memory, at least for dreams, and the interest and courage to look within and to record what he found there, however dimly understood. He wrote approximately 134 dream poems, on four major and six minor themes. Granted that some of these poems are simply titled "recording a dream" (*ji-meng*) and are indistinguishable from other poems on similar themes, many of them have quite long and detailed titles relating the dream experience, and most of them evoke a dreamlike mood in their style and presentation.[2]

The major and minor themes treated in these poems and the

132

number of poems relating to each are as follows: Daoist philosophy (alchemy, immortality, seclusion, including two that employ largely Buddhist imagery): thirty-nine; travel or landscape: twenty-three; friendship (generally meeting dead friends, and drinking and exchanging poems with them): twenty-three; heroic-patriotic: twenty-two; personal lament and sadness at his fate and lack of accomplishments: nine; nostalgia (for his home while in Sichuan, and for Sichuan after his return home and retirement, including at least four poems about his first love Tang Wan): nine; drinking: five; studies: two; and one each on the art of poetry and on a particular landscape painting. As we have come to expect, Daoism and nature come first, with almost twice as many poems on Daoist themes, primarily the quest for immortality, as any other. As he grew older, his dreams were almost exclusively concerned with Daoist immortality and his memories of departed friends. An observation of Jung's seems to apply quite well to Lu: "In old age one begins to let memories unroll before the mind's eye and, musing, to recognize oneself in the inner and outer images of the past. This is like a preparation for an existence in the hereafter, just as, in Plato's view, philosophy is a preparation for death."[3] I have selected a representative sampling of Lu's dream poems on the themes mentioned above, primarily Daoist in nature and most of them written after his retirement.

"Song of the Divine Prince" was "written while visiting (Prince) Ying Xian's Temple" in Shu-zhou at the age of forty-eight. The poem is couched in a very free Ancient Verse form, basically seven characters per line, but with occasional lines of four, five, nine and two characters.[4] Prince Ying Xian was the local deity of Zi-tong or Tong-*xian* in Zi-zhou. According to ancient records he was originally the son of one Zhang Ya (or Wu) of the Jin dynasty, but Professor Eberhard states that he can also be called Zhang Ya and that he was closely connected with the temple oracles and shamanism.[5] He was said to have served the Jin dynasty and to have died in battle, for which he was awarded a temple (*miao*). During the Tang dynasty, when the Bright Emperor (Ming Huang) was hunting in Sichuan, this deity met him at the Wan-li Bridge. Ming Huang then made him a posthumous left prime minister (*zuo cheng-xiang*).

After that time, he made several miraculous appearances to aid
emperors and generals, and each time he was given a higher
office; finally, he was raised to the rank of prince (*wang*).

> Mount Tai could become a pebble,
> The Eastern Sea turn into dust—
> Only a brave warrior's ambition
> 4 Must be fulfilled in life or death.
> I dreamed the Divine Prince descended from Heaven,
> His awesome bearing, grand, magnificent, hard to
>      fully recount;
> Not horses but flying dragons pulled his chariot,
> 8 While ghosts and spirits shouted before and yelled behind!
> Strange shapes and freakish forms,
> Thick as fish scales,
> Paired horns bobbing wildly,
> 12 Struggled to support the chariot wheels.
> Black flags and white banners
> Came down without end.
> Yellow mists and purple miasmas
> 16 Joined and scattered in twisting spirals.
> Mountain goblins, suffering interrogation,
> Screamed, shouted, moaned, and groaned!
> Paired dragons, bound and tied,
> 20 Coiled up in tame submission.
> A hundred more chariots followed carrying beautiful women;
> Scarves and robes fresh and lovely, coquettish their smiles.
> Gold goblets and turquoise dippers overflowed with sweet wine;
> 24 Lutes, guitars, and horizontal harps inlaid with rare jewels.
> Human life, short and cramped, is full of bitter sadness;
> Divine Prince's happiness and joy will last a million springs.
> Alas!
> In life not made a noble, in death given a temple—
> 28 How could such a man of real ambition long remain silent!

The first four lines and the final two lines of the poem express
the basic theme that a "brave warrior's ambition" (*zhuang-shi
zhi*) is bound to be fulfilled in heroic acts performed either in
life or after death. Lu found it not at all surprising that Ying
Xian did not "long remain silent" (*chang mo-mo*). There is an
obvious reference to himself here in that his own dream, as

expressed in the poem "Expressing My Ambition" on page 78 above, was to be fulfilled after his death even though frustrated in life. Lines five to twenty-six describe Lu's dream of Ying Xian descending from Heaven employing a series of otherworldly images and a forceful depiction of color and action reminiscent of Li Bo's famous poem "Song of a Dream Visit to Tian-mu."[6] The picture Lu provides here is so detailed, in fact, and the theme so characteristic of his patriotic verse, that one may perhaps doubt if this long poem is really a record of an actual dream.

"Dream of Immortals," a five character Regulated poem, has a prose preface:[7]

I dreamed I was in the morning audience at the Palace of Great Officers. Looking up, it was very near to Heaven and the stars were all as large as the moon. The weather was clear and cold as in the tenth month [early winter], but it was really the first day of the second month [midspring] of the *geng-zi* year [1180, Lu was fifty-four].

> At midnight I roamed the imperial realm—
> A vast palace peopled with immortal officers.
> Near to Heaven the starry hosts loomed large;
> 4 In clear frost their jewelled swords were cold.
> I wrote poems upon jade-green tablets,
> Attended banquets riding a blue phoenix.
> Sadly disappointed my dust-bound fate's so heavy—
> 8 The dream has ended, but the night's not yet over!

The "Palace of Great Officers" (*da-guan-dian*) appears to be Lu You's own invention, but *da-guan* refers to the Son of Heaven—the emperor. "Immortal officers" (*xian-guan*) are mentioned in the *Biographies of Holy Immortals* (*shen-xian-zhuan*) and other similar books as famous men who have become divine officers in the Heavenly Court. Sometimes they were put in charge of the four directions or made guardians of particular areas on earth. Lu's return from dreams of immortality are always sadly sobering.

"Recording a Dream of the Twenty-third Night of the Fifth Month" is a seven character Ancient Verse poem written at the age of sixty-nine.[8]

Night clepsydra nearly drained, cocks beginning to crow,
I dreamed of a divine immortal, believe it not illusory.
Stream flow pounded down emerald valley floor;
4 Pine roots wound across cobalt cliffsides.
Slowly walking the forest edge I came to a flying bridge,
Overhanging thousand yard steep cliffs with startling waves.
Not only treading dangerous heights caused my feet to stumble;
8 Already sensing the secluded place my spirits grew still.
Empty grotto waters dripped, in time transformed to stone—
Jewelled canopies and pearl rosaries imaged in worldly objects.
Ghosts and demons, dark and menacing, seemed about to fight;
12 Dragons and serpents, creeping and crawling, who'd dare pass?
Long-eyebrowed, old transcendent riding the white clouds,
Took my hand, gave me a green jade staff:
"In three births you had a world-transcending destiny—
16 With one thought cut through dust-laden delusions!
Although it's said past events are not again recalled,
I'm moved that your eyes' divine glow is still bright.
Why wait any longer for gold and cinnabar to ripen?
20 Follow me, return and dwell in Mount Kun's Garden!"

In this dream Lu seems to have journeyed to a Daoist "grotto heaven" ("empty grotto," *kong-yan*) where he met a hoary Daoist immortal (*lao-xian*) who told him of his "world-transcending destiny" (*shi-wai-yuan*) and invited him to go with him to live in the Chinese Elysium, "Mount Kun's Garden" (*kun-lang*) on Mount Kun Lun. The imagery is basically Buddhist, except for the mention of a divine glow" (*shen*) in his eyes (literally, "pupils" *tong*), achieved through Daoist style meditation. In lines nine and ten the stalactites and stalagmites seen in the cave are described as providing the models for the magnificent "jewelled canopies" (*bao-gai*) seen behind Buddhas in Buddhist iconography and the "pearl rosaries" (*zhu-ying*) used in Buddhist worship. The "three births" (*san-sheng*) refer to the Buddhist concept of past, present, and future incarnations. "One thought" (*yi-nian*) means "one concentration of mind," in which one reaches enlightenment by seeing through the "delusions" (*zhang*) of the "dust" (*chen*)—the illusory world of sensations.[9]

The next poem is similar to the "An Qi Chapter" poem on pages 83–84 above in that it deals with a dream of ingesting a magic herb of immortality. "I Dreamed Someone Gave Me Foxglove, the flavor was sweet as honey, playfully I wrote a few words to record the event" is a five character Ancient Verse poem written at the age of sixty-nine, just after his recovery from an eighteen day illness.[10]

> A traveller giving out foxglove,
> Opened his case:
> Startling, extraordinary wonder!
> I hastily took it and chewed it up;
> 4  No time for further decoction.
> Strange scent penetrated Kun Lun.
> Pure waters produced a Jade Pool.
> Fantastic flavor cannot be named,
> 8  Far surpassing "sweet as honey."
> Young children joyfully told this old man,
> His snowy cheeks sprouted black whiskers!
> Age and sickness lost their abode!
> 12  Just about to discard my staff and run,
> Dawn cocks called me from dream to waking!
> Teeth and mouth still rich with lingering sweetness,
> I send this message to mountain-dwelling friends:
> 16  You need no longer seek magic gold and mushrooms!

"Foxglove," or "Earth Yellow" (*di-huang*) in Chinese, is a tall plant with purple or white flowers like glove fingers (*Rehmannia lutea*). It is said to possess many of the miraculous powers attributed to the more familiar ginseng root (*ren-shen*). Actually, true foxglove has no fragrance, is used as a drug (digitalis) for heart trouble, and, if too much consumed results in death. Its functions are quite different from ginseng, and Lu was probably dealing with some other as yet unidentified herb in this poem. At any rate, the effect described here is the usual one of rejuvenation. Lines five and six are a symbolic description of the fact that the fragrance of the herb "penetrates" (*tou*) his brain (*Kun Lun*) and the taste causes him to salivate profusely, thus producing a "Jade Pool" (*yu-chi*) in his mouth. If the herb tasted anything like peyote or other psychedelics, this would be a common reaction. "Mountain-dwelling friends" (*shan-zhong-you*) are, of course, recluses seeking immortality by means of ingesting alchemical gold and "magic mushrooms" (*zhi*, actually the purple polypore fungus), believed to confer longevity or immortality because of their remarkable resistance to decay.[11]

"Recording a Dream of the Twenty-fourth Night of the Eleventh Month of the *wu-wu* Year" [1198, Lu was seventy-three] is a seven character Ancient Verse poem that describes a dream in which Lu was taken for an "aged transcendent" (*lao-xian*) by the customers of a wine shop.[12]

> South lane wine shop glowed vermilion and green;
> Mile wide lake luster reflected mountain colors.
> I came half drunk, climbing the lofty staircase,
> 4 In low hat, long sash, and yellow cotton robe.
> Followed by a mountain boy carrying medicine bags.
> Seated guests looked startled hearing flying clogs:
> "We've lately heard an aged transcendent passed this way—
> 8 Might be this old man; who can tell?"
> They stepped back, invited me in, bowed and saluted,
> Strove to offer fine wine, hoping for the dregs.
> About to explain myself, I knew they wouldn't listen,
> 12 Just went on smiling and took the seat of honor.
> Let go a lofty discourse, startling them all!
> Before I knew nearby cock-crow shattered my dream!
> Whenever men fool themselves it's usually like this—
> 16 I chant this poem on my pillow to recall my faults.

His hosts salute him with great politeness and formality and offer him "goblets of fine wine" (*ming-zun*) "hoping for the dregs" (*ji-yu-li*) in order to drink from the same cup that an immortal has used and thereby gain some of his longevity magic. Lu wanted at first to explain himself, but he knew that they would not believe him, so he played the role to the hilt by taking the best seat and "letting go a lofty discourse that startled them all" (*gao-tan fang-zong jing si-zuo*). Upon waking, he muses that he and they were only "fooling themselves" (*zi-qi*), believing that there are such immortals and that one might meet one or even become one. Surely such ideas are only the stuff of dreams.

"Recording a Dream," a seven character Ancient Verse poem

written at eighty-three, describes an experience similar to many referred to in William James's *Varieties of Religious Experience,* in which, under the influence of "laughing gas" or some other drug, one believes he has discovered the secret of the universe, but upon awakening the whole idea is completely forgotten.[13] In this dream Lu met an old master in a paradisical realm who showed him some mystical writings, which he hastily copied down. He thought he would not forget them, but of course he did.

> Dream-roaming a strange realm I could not recognize—
> Turquoise cliffs and azure crags rose a thousand feet.
> A storied terrace, mist-enshrouded, loomed above them;
> 4 Waving my arms I flew skyward even without wings.
> On the gate was a flat plaque written in eight parts,
> With wondrous force quite unlike normal human script.
> The host, in deerskin cap and purple silk robe,
> 8 Was happy to receive me as a long lost friend;
> Opened his vest, showed me some pages of writing—
> Marvelous lines of mysterious words, all in superior style.
> I hastily copied them down in a most uncertain hand;
> 12 My host, ruffled and rattled, seemed quite begrudging.
> In dreaming once again I knew it was a dream,
> Feared upon waking there'd be nowhere to look.
> Reckoned I could remember well, would not forget;
> 16 At cock-crow dream-returning, vainly heaved a sigh!

The final poem to be cited is one that Lu wrote in the tenth month of 1209 at the age of eighty-four, while on his deathbed. At the time he had less than four months to live. The full title of this seven character Regulated Verse poem is, "On the Twenty-fourth Night of the Tenth Month I Dreamed of Escorting the Daoist Master of Mount Lu back [on his return, *gui*] to Mount Lu."[14] "Return to the mountains" (*gui-shan*) is an obvious reference to death.

> My whole life I never entered the three great offices;
> In last years returning home to Five Elders Temple.
> Old scholars know well success comes after appointment;
> 4 My generation relied on that as our guiding principle.

Lone boat moored at night, rapids sound menacing.
Little jug fragment at dawn, snow feels cold.
Laughingly converse at bedside leaning on our staffs—
8  With me today you alone retain a like awareness.


The first half of the poem describes his official life as one of
failure and frustration; while the second half describes his journey toward Mount Lu, a famous Buddhist and Daoist retreat in
Jiangxi Province, and his enlightenment. "The three great offices"
(*san-gong*) refer to high court offices during the Zhou dynasty,
and the line means that he never held a high office at court and
could never influence the emperor. The "Five Elders Temple"
(*wu-lao-an*) was located on "Five Elders Mountain," which
formed the southern slope of Mount Lu. The first couplet means,
then, that Lu retired without ever having achieved any great
success. The second couplet elaborates on that theme by stat-
ing that he worked hard all of his life to achieve a court appointment. The third couplet turns to the trip down the river to
Mount Lu in the winter. The water is perhaps shallow and thus
the rapids are dangerous, but they can take some comfort in
warm morning wine. The final couplet not only resolves the
problem posed in the first half of the poem, as a correct regulated poem should do, but it portrays Lu and the Daoist master
happily putting to rest the so-called problem of life by reaching
a "like awareness" (*tong-can*) of the Way. *Can* is a technical
term in both Daoism and Buddhism that implies transcendence
of and liberation from normal human perceptions and worldly
cares by "understanding," "penetrating," or "seeing through"
(*can* is most often paired with *tou*, "to penetrate") surface reality
into the essential nature of the Way of nature (*Dao*). It was by
having the "same awareness" that these two men, and since this
is a dream they must both be identified with Lu himself, "have
a link with the infinite." By this time Lu had learned the answer
to what Jung called "the decisive question for man:"[15]

The decisive question for man is: Is he related to something
infinite or not? That is the telling question of his life. Only if we
know that the thing which truly matters is the infinite [for Lu, the
*Dao*] can we avoid fixing our interest upon futilities, and upon all

kinds of goals which are not of real importance [for Lu, success in office, lines one to four]. Thus we demand that the world grant us recognition for qualities which we regard as personal possessions: our talent or our beauty. The more a man lays stress on false possessions, and the less sensitivity he has for what is essential, the less satisfying is his life. He feels limited because he has limited aims, and the result is envy and jealousy. If we understand and feel that here in this life we already have a link with the infinite [*Dao*], desires and attitudes change. In the final analysis, we count for something only because of the essential [*Dao*] we embody, and if we do not embody that, life is wasted. In our relationships to other men, too, the crucial question is whether the element of boundlessness [the *Zhuang Zi*'s "roaming beyond the bounds"] is expressed in the relationship.

Secure in his answer, arrived at after many years of spiritual quest and often represented in his poetry, Lu was ready to "return."

# Notes and References

All references to Lu You's work are to the *Shi-jie shu-ju* edition in two volumes. Printed in Taipei in 1963 and entitled *Lu Fang-weng quan-ji* (Complete Works), it is a paginated version of the standard *Si-bu bei-yao* (Essentials of the Four Libraries) edition. All translated materials have been checked with the latter edition. References to his poetic collection, the *Jian-nan shi-gao*, are given thus: *juan* number/page number/romanization of part or all of the title. References to his prose collection, the *Wei-nan wen-ji*, are the same except that they are preceded by a W/. All references to the twenty-five standard histories are by the name and chapter number (example: *Jin-shu*, 49) and are to the well-known *Kai-ming shu-dian* edition printed in Shanghai in 1935. Other abbreviations used in these notes are explained below.

### Abbreviations of Frequently Cited Works

| | |
|---|---|
| JNSG | *Jian-nan shi-gao* (as mentioned above) |
| LFWSCX | *Lu Fang-weng shi-ci-xuan.* |
| LXABJ | *Lao-xue-an bi-ji.* |
| LYPZ | *Lu You ping-zhuan.* |
| LYSX | *Lu You shi-xuan.* |
| LYYJ | *Lu You yan-jiu.* |

Soothill and Hodous, *Dictionary*, refers to William E. Soothill and Lewis Hodous *A Dictionary of Chinese Buddhist Terms*, London: Kegan Paul, Trench, Trubner, and Co., Ltd., n.d.

### Chapter One

1. See Michael S. Duke, "The Life and Works of Lu You (1125–1210)" (Ph.D. dissertation, University of California, Berkeley, 1975 [available from University Microfilms, Ann Arbor, Michigan]), pp. 1–197, for a complete biography based on Lu's poetry and prose and the modern Chinese biographical studies mentioned in the bibliography.

2. C.G. Jung, *Memories, Dreams, Reflections,* trans. Richard and Clara Winston (New York, 1961–63) pp. 44–45.

3. W/27/165 *Ba Li zhuang-jian-gong jia-shu* (1188).

143

4. 1/3 *Ye du bing-shu.*

5. 3/43–44 *Shan-nan xing.*

6. See pp. 71–76 for Zhu-ge Liang.

7. 85/1153 *Shi-er.* The "Nine Islands" (*jiu-zhou*) is an ancient term for China and the "Central Plains" (*zhong-yuan*) are the northern areas.

8. Lin Hui-ling, "Lu Fang-Weng de li-hun," in Liang Rong-ruo, ed., *Wen-xue shi-jia-zhuan,* (Taizhong, 1966) pp. 281–82.

9. Professor Wolfram Eberhard of the University of California wrote me that a short part of the text of the play *Chai-tou-feng* is in a book called *Guo-xi ji-cheng,* p. 195; but I have been unable to find it.

10. Personal communication from Wolfram Eberhard.

11. *Ibid.*

12. 14/234 *Shi-yue er-shi-liu-ri.* . . .

13. 14/245 *Cao-shu ge.*

14. *Jin-shu,* 43.

15. Richard Wilhelm and Cary F. Baynes, *The I Ching, or Book of Changes,* (Princeton, 1950 and 1967), p. 15.

16. W/26/157 *Ba si-ma zi-wei er song ju fa.* . .

17. 1/18 *Ye du yin-shu you-gan.*

18. See Joseph Needham, et al. *Science and Civilization in China,* vol. II (Cambridge, 1962), pp. 139–54.

19. The Zhang-ren Guan was established during the Jin dynasty on the spot where the Yellow Ancestor (*huang-di*) was said to have built an altar to Ning Feng, who was also known as the Sage of the Five Peaks (*wu-yue zhang-ren*).

20. 72/996 *Yu qing-you qing-cheng.* . . Lines nine and ten allude to a story in the *Lie Zi, Shuo-fu* chapter, the point of which is the same as that made in lines seven and eight: one must study the Way with singleminded determination and not in a dilettantish manner.

21. 26/433 *Ji-shan nong.* Mount Ji is Kuai-ji-shan south of Lu's home in Shanyin, Shao-xing–*xian,* Zhejiang.

22. *LYSX,* p. 148.

23. *Ibid,* p. 149.

24. 69/965 *Shi-yi-yue nian-qi-ri.* . .

25 Burton Watson, *The Complete Works of Chuang Tzu* (New York, 1968), p. 78.

26. *Ibid.,* p. 368.

27. *Ibid.,* pp. 315–16, italics added.

28. *Ibid.*

29. *LYYJ,* ch. 3, "Lu You zai nong-cun," pp. 31–34 especially.

Professor Wolfram Eberhard, who pointed out several errors in my dissertation on these points, is inclined to agree with Zhu.

30. Jung, p. 359, italics added.

31. 85/1150 *Shen-yin.*

32. Watson, pp. 39, 41, 44–45, and 48–49, italics added.

## Chapter Two

1. *Ba jian-nan shi-gao,* on p. 1155 just after chapter 85.

2. 25/418 *Jiu-yue yi-ri ye du shi-gao you-gan...*

3. Soothill and Hodous, *Dictionary,* pp. 66a and 254b.

4. See my article, "The Loom of Creation: Lu You's View of the Art of Poetry," *Literature East and West* (forthcoming).

5. *San-guo-zhi,* 21 and *Jin-shu,* 49.

6. 54/778 *Ru-qiu you-shan fu-shi...* No. 1.

7. 78/1076 *Shi Zi-yu.*

8. Arthur Waley, *The Analects of Confucius* (New York, 1938), p. 229.

9. Burton Watson, trans., *Introduction to Sung Poetry.* (Yoshikawa Kojiro's *Soshi Gaisetsu*) (Cambridge, Mass., 1967), pp. 138–39.

10. *LXABJ* 4/25–26. Translations of Tao Yuan-ming are from James Robert Hightower, *The Poetry of T'ao Ch'ien* (Oxford, 1970), pp. 130 and 268–70.

11. *LYYJ,* pp. 95–103, presents all of the poems and prose pieces relevant to Zeng Ji.

12. 16/274 *Da Zheng Yu-ren "jian-fa" jian-zeng,* lines 9–12. Lü Ju-ren is quoted in *LYYJ,* p. 109.

13. *LYPZ,* pp. 363–64 presents a large selection of Lu's poems mentioning the *Songs.*

14. 73/1008 *Du bin-feng.*

15. 2/25 *Ai-ying,* two poems.

16. David Hawkes, *Ch'u Tz'u, The Songs of the South* (Boston, 1962) pp. 59–69 and 65–67.

17. *Ibid.,* p. 66.

18. *LYPZ,* pp. 359–60, presents many poems mentioning Qu Yuan and the *Li Sao.*

19. W/17/100–01 *Dong-tun gao-zhai ji.* See A. R. Davis, *Tu Fu* (New York, 1971), pp. 70–71, 93, 110, 114–15, 123 and 90–95, for the incidents mentioned. 'Jing Ke, the would-be assassin of the first emperor, sang and wept with his friends before setting off on his ill-fated mission. Ruan Ji, a melancholy poet of the late Han, was said to have often ordered his servant to drive him as fast

as possible along a deserted road until it came to an end, whereupon
he would weep uncontrollably.

20. *LYPZ,* pp. 349–55, presents many poems mentioning Du Fu,
as well as a selection of poems using lines from Du's verse.

21. Davis, pp. 67–97.

22. 2/36 *Ye deng Bai-di-cheng-lou.* . .

23. See David Hawkes, *A Little Primer of Tu Fu* (Oxford, 1907),
pp. 200–202.

24. *LXABJ*/7/47–48. The translation is mine. Compare Hawkes,
*A Little Primer of Tu Fu,* p. 209. The book mentioned here was an
anthology of poems in two chapters exchanged (*chou-chang*) by
Yang Yi, Liu Yun, Qian Wei-yan, and others who imitated exclusively the poetry of Li Shang-yin and delighted in the use of "abstruse
allusions" (*pi-dian*) and ambiguous diction.

25. 70/975 *Du Li Du shi.*

26. *LYSX,* p. 237.

27. 7/109 *Jin-ting.*

28. *Han-shu,* 89, "*Huang Ba zhuan,*" ("The Biography of Huang
Ba").

29. 14/244 *Zui-ge.*

30. Edward H. Schafer, *Ancient China* (New York, 1967), p. 14.

31. *LYPZ,* pp. 355–59, lists many poems mentioning Tao and using
lines from his verse.

32. 26/425 *Song-xia zong-bi.*

33. *Sou-shen-ji,* Shanghai: Commercial Press, 1937.

34. 27/443 *Du Tao shi.*

35. Arthur Waley, *Yuan Mei* (New York, n.d. [1956]), pp. 153–54.

36. 68/949 *Yu yu-zuo bu-zhi pu-kou.*

37. Hawkes, *Ch'u Tz'u,* p. 90.

38. Waley, *Analects,* p. 103.

39. 80/1094 *Du Tao shi.* Hightower, p. 229.

40. W/15/84 *Mei Sheng-yu bie-ji xu.*

41. 60/855 *Du Yuan-ling xian-sheng shi.*

42. Watson, *Introduction to Sung Poetry,* pp. 72–78.

43. *Ibid.,* p. 75.

44. Watson, *Chuang Tzu,* pp. 50–51.

45. 62/882 *Qiu-huai* No. 4.

46. 84/1139 *Jia-ding ji-si,* l. 1.

47. 64/906 *You-xing.*

48. Hightower, p. 269.

49. 2/27 *Jiang li jiang-ling,* ll. 9 and 10.

50. 80/1089 *Zuo-xue han-shen you-fu.*

### Chapter Three

1. Zhao Yi's *Ou-bei shi-hua* is quoted in *LYPZ*, pp. 333–34 and *LYYJ*, p. 113.

2. Liang Qi-chao, "*Du Lu Fang-weng ji-shi*," in *Yin-bing-shi wen-ji*, quoted in *LYPZ*, p. 334.

3. Jacques Gernet, *Daily Life in China on the Eve of the Mongol Invasion, 1250–1276* (Palo Alto, 1970), p. 247.

4. 4/67 *Guan da-san-guan-tu you-gan*.

5. 16/272 *Gan-fen*.

6. See Burton Watson, *Early Chinese Literature* (New York, 1962), pp. 17–120.

7. 9/157 *You Zhu-ge wu-hou shu-tai*.

8. *LYSX*, pp. 74–75.

9. 4/70 *Hu wu-ren*.

10. Quoted in *LFWSCX*, p. 39.

11. *Shi-ji*, ch. 109, translated by Burton Watson in Cyril Birch, ed., *Anthology of Chinese Literature*, vol. 1 (New York, 1965), pp. 123–33.

12. *LYSX* and *LFWSCX* both mention these two references.

13. The similarity to the first lines of *The East is Red* (*dong-fang hong*) is so striking I could not help mentioning it.

14. The last three characters of line eighteen, *peng-chuang deng*, "reed window lamp," are not translated; instead I've added "scholar," for which they are a metonym, to contrast with the martial hero of the poem.

15. 4/66 *Bao-jian yin*.

16. 7/114 *Song ji xing*.

17. Davis, pp. 141 and 144.

18. 35/546 *Shu-zhi*.

19. It is typical of the editorial practices of Communist critics that they explain the allusion to Su Wu, a Confucian, but they do not explain this equally important allusion to a Daoist (hence "negative") classic.

20. *LYSX* and *LFWSCX*, pp. 178–80 and 162–63 respectively.

21. 77/1054 *Yi-meng*.

### Chapter Four

1. Robert De Ropp, *The Master Game* (New York, 1968), p. 20.

2. Max Kaltenmark, *Le Lie-Sien Tchouan*, p. 18, quoted in Mircea Eliade, *The Forge and the Crucible* (New York, n.d. [1956 and 1962]), pp. 109–10.

3. W/26/155 *Ba xiu-xin jian.* "Roam beyond the realm" (*you fang-wai*) is from the *Zhuang Zi* and refers to Daoists in general.

4. *LXABJ* 5/31. My translation is based on that in Ho-peng Yoke et al., *Lu Yu, the Poet Alchemist* (Canberra, 1972), pp. 8–9.

5. Personal communication from Professor Wolfram Eberhard.

6. 16/282 *An Qi pian.*

7. Needham, p. 134, note b.

8. The *Zhou Li* (*Rites of Zhou,* an idealized picture of Zhou dynasty government) says that the five clouds were observed in the skies in order to predict good and evil fortunes.

9. Eliade, p. 118.

10. 16/286 *Kun lun xing.*

11. Eliade, pp. 117–18, quoting Rolf Stein, *Jardins en miniature d'Extreme-Orient,* p. 54.

12. Alan W. Watts, *Psychotherapy East and West* (New York, 1961), pp. 39–40, quoting Ludwig Wittgenstein, *Tractatus Logico-Philosophicus,* (London, 1960), sections 6.5, 6.51, 6.52, and 6.521.

13. W/49/301 *Hao shi jin* No. 6.

14. The *Zhuang Zi,* ch. 2; see Watson, *Chuang Tzu,* p. 43. Goethe's poem "Epirrhema" is excerpted in Theodore Roszak, ed., *Where the Wasteland Ends, Political Transcendence in Postindustrial Society* (Garden City, N. Y., 1973), p. 316.

15. Watts, pp. 57–58, quoting E. Cassirer, *Substance and Function and Einstein's Theory of Relativity* (New York, 1953), p. 398.

16. See Needham, pp. 99–100, "the return to cooperative primitivity," and pp. 100–102, "the attack on feudalism," for the social and political aspects of the perception of a state of undifferentiated *hundun.*

17. See the *Chu Elegies* poem "Summons of the Soul" (*zhao-hun*) in Hawkes, *Ch'u Tz'u.*

18. Norman O. Brown, in Theodore Roszak, ed., *Sources* (New York, 1972), p. 459.

19. Soothill and Hodous, *Dictionary,* pp. 422 and 432.

20. 26/433 *Bi-shi-xing.*

21. Watson, *Chuang Tzu,* pp. 316–17.

22. *Ibid.,* p. 327.

23. Renato Poggioli, "The Oaten Flute," in *Perspectives on Poetry,* eds. James L. Calderwood and Harold E. Toliver (New York: Oxford University Press, 1968), p. 224, quoted in Irving Yucheng Lo, *Hsin Ch'i-chi* (New York, 1971), p. 75.

24. Stanley Diamond, "The Search for the Primitive," *Man's Image in Medicine and Anthropology,* Galdston, ed. (New York, 1963), quoted in Roszak, *Sources,* p. 233.

25. *Dao De Jing*, chapter 18. This book, also known as the *Lao Zi*, has been translated by Arthur Waley as *The Way and Its Power* (Boston and New York, 1935).

26. Roszak, pp. 212–36.

27. 80/1089 *Hu-shan xun-mei* No. 1.

28. Arthur Waley, *The Nine Songs* (London, 1955), pp. 23–25.

29. Watson, *Chuang Tzu*, pp. 32–33, and p. 327.

30. 63/891 *Du wang muo-jie, . . . jie wu-wai shi ye* No. 7.

31. Needham, pp. 434–41.

32. *Ibid.*, pp. 116–17.

33. Watson, *Chuang Tzu*, p. 244.

34. 54/777 *Yang-sheng.*

35. D. T. Suzuki, *An Introduction to Zen Buddhism* (New York, 1964), p. 86.

36. See "Written During a Late Spring Rain," in Duke, p. 331; 57/833 *Chun-wan yu-zhong zuo.*

37. 57/813 *Dao-shi shu-huai.*

38. Needham, p. 144.

39. 76/1053 *Shu-zhong bei-chuang zhou-wo you-zuo.*

40. D. C. Lau, *Mencius* (Harmondsworth, 1970), p. 165.

41. Soothill and Hodous, *Dictionary*, p. 255.

### Chapter Five

1. 9/144 *Jiang-lou zui-zhong zuo.*

2. *Jin-shu*, ch. 49. Chen Shou-yi, *Chinese Literature* (New York, 1963), p. 157.

3. A phrase from Tao's "Drinking Poem No. 14," in Hightower, p. 145.

4. 13/228 *Dui-jiu*, ll. 1–10 only, the rest being patriotic lament.

5. 17/306 *Cheng-qi kan-shan yin-jiu*, ll. 1–4.

6. 34/526 *Chun-su*, ll. 3–4.

7. 67/936 *She-yin.*

8. Hightower, p. 143.

9. 81/1109 *Jiu-shou shu-xi.*

10. 5/80 *Tong He Yuan-li shang he-hua. . .* , ll. 1–2. Burton Watson, *The Old Man Who Does As He Pleases* (New York, 1973), p. 13, has a complete translation.

11. 7/111 *Shu-huai*, ll. 5–6; flowers may again refer to young ladies.

12. 7/117 *He-jiang ye-yan gui ma-shang zuo*, ll. 3–4.

13. 16/286 *Cun-yin*, ll. 1–4.

14. 38/586 *Dui-jiu*, ll. 7–8; Long River is the Yangzi.

15. 52/760 *Xia-ri nong-bi xi-shu*, ll. 1–4.
16. "Drinking Poem No. 7," l. 3, in Hightower, pp. 133–34.
17. 8/27 *Lou-shang zui-shu*.
18. *Jin-shu*, ch. 43.
19. 5/82 *Yin-jiu*.
20. 7/112 *Dui-jiu*.
21. 4/65 *Zui-ge*.
22. 4/75 *Chi-shang zui-ge*. Compare translation in Yoke, pp. 12–14.
23. *Ibid.*, p. 13.
24. *Shi-ji*, 6. "*Qin shi-huang ji,*" ("Records of the first emperor of the Qin dynasty").
25. *Li Sao*, l. 98, in Hawkes, *Ch'u Tz'u*, p. 28, n. 6.
26. 25/422 *Zui-dao-ge*.
27. Hightower, p. 139.
28. 30/479 *Zui-ge*.
29. 41/617 *Wu-jiu-tan*.

*Chapter Six*

1. 2/31 *Qu-tang xing*.
2. 53/773 *Zhou-xing qian-qing ke-qiao zhi jian*.
3. Watson, *Introduction to Sung Poetry*, p. 47.
4. 3/57 *Jia-yang guan-she qi-shi shen-fu*. . .
5. Jung, p. 42.
6. Watson, *Chuang Tzu*, pp. 75–76.
7. 33/514 *Deng dong-shan*.
8. Arthur Waley, *Book of Songs* No. 79. This song is No. 22 in the standard Chinese version of the *Songs* known as the *Mao-shi*.
9. Watson, *Introduction to Sung Poetry*, pp. 34–35, has a translation of 50/727 *Mei-hua jue-ju* No. 3 and a discussion of Lu's different usage of an idea from a poem by Liu Zong-yuan of the Tang dynasty.
10. James J. Y. Liu, *The Poetry of Li Shang-yin* (Chicago, 1969), p. 160.
11. 61/871 *Chu-xia xian-bu cun-luo-jian*.
12. 5/80–81 *Yi-zhai*.
13. 10/161–62 *Zui-zhong xia qu-tang-xia, zhong-liu guan shi-bi fei-quan*.
14. 3/41 *Yue-chi nong-jia*.
15. 20/348 *Qi-yue shi-ri dao gu-shan*. . . *zi-shi*.
16. "Beat a drum" is a free translation of *ji-rang*, which could mean "pound on the ground," except that the commentaries identify *rang* as a musical instrument made of earth or wood said to have

been used by the old men who sang the *di-li* song translated in the text.

17. 37/567 *Dong-xi-jia.*
18. 29/461 *Sai-shen-qu.* Professor Wolfram Eberhard gave me a good deal of information on this festival.
19. 33/516–17 *Xiao-zhou you jin-cun, she-zhou bu-gui.*
20. Hightower, pp. 254–58.
21. Liu Wu-chi, *An Introduction to Chinese Literature* (Bloomington, 1966), pp. 247–52.
22 40/610 *Mu-niu-er.*
23. 43/642 *A-mu.*
24. 66/966 *Fan-zhou jin-jia-geng zeng mai-xin Wang-weng.*
25. 32/502 *Nong-jia-tan.*

### Chapter Seven

1. *LYPZ,*, pp. 333–34.
2. See, for example, the titles to dream poems on pages 98, 142, 243, 520, 533, and 845 in the *JNSG*, as well as the longer titles translated here.
3. Jung, p. 320.
4. 5/79 *Shen-jun-ge, ye Ying Xian miao zuo.*
5. Personal communication from Wolfram Eberhard.
6. Translated in Burton Watson, *Chinese Lyricism* (New York, 1971), pp. 150–53.
7. 12/206 *Meng-xian.*
8. 32/510 *Wu-yue er-shi-san-ye ji-meng.*
9. Soothill and Hodous, *Dictionary*, pp. 70, 6, 429, 422, 478, and 330.
10. 33/512 *Meng you xiang di-huang zhe...*
11. Schafer, p. 63.
12. 38/586 *Ji wu-wu shi-yi-yue er-shi-si-ye meng.* I have placed line four in the original in the sixth place and moved lines five and six up to fourth and fifth place.
13. 77/1058 *Ji-meng.* See: William James, *The Varieties of Religious Experience* (New York, 1911).
14. 85/1150 *Shi-yue er-shi-si-ye meng-zhong song Lu shan dao-ren gui-shan.*
15. Jung, p. 325.

# Selected Bibliography

### Works in Chinese and Japanese

A. Editions of Lu's Works (in chronological order)

LU YOU, *Lu-Fang-weng quan-ji*, 6 vols., *Si-bu bei-yao*, Taiwan: *Zhong-hua shu-ju*, n.d. This edition is based on that of the Ming dynasty bibliophile Mao Jin. There are no commentaries.

————, *Jian-nan shi-chao*, 6 vols., Shanghai: *Sao-ye-shan-fang*, 1914. A selection of "three parts in ten" of Lu's poetry with a preface by Yang Da-he dated 1685.

————, *Jing-xuan Lu Fang-weng shi-ji* 2 vols., *Si-bu cong-kan*, Shanghai: *Han-fen-lou*, 1922. An "essential selection" of Lu's poems reprinted from a Ming dynasty edition owned by a Mr. Liu of Wu-xing.

————, *Wei-nan wen-ji*, 12 vols., *Si-bu cong-kan*, Shanghai: *Han-fen lou*, 1922. Lu's entire prose collection reprinted from a Ming dynasty edition owned by a Mr. Hua of Jiang-nan.

JI FENG, ed. *Lu Fang-weng shi-ci-xuan*, Hangzhou: *Zhejiang ren-min chu-ban-she*, 1957. The most balanced of the mainland anthologies.

YOU GUO-EN and LI YI, eds. *Lu You shi-xuan*, Peking: *Ren-min wen-xue chu-ban-she*, 1957.

LU YOU, *Lu Fang-weng quan-ji*, Taipei: *Shi-jie shu-ju*, 1963. A two volume edition of the first reference above with some additional materials and with page numbers.

TANG JI-CHUN, ed. *Lu You shi-ci xuan-shi*, Hong Kong: *Wan-li shu-dian*, 1963.

HUANG YI-ZHI, ed. *Lu You shi*, Taipei: Commercial Press 1970.


B. Chronology, Biography, and Criticism (alphabetical order)

DI ZHAN-NA, *Fang-weng ci yan-jiu*, Taipei: publisher unlisted, 1970.

KAWAKAMI HAJIME, *Riku Ho-o kan-sho*, 2 vols., Kyoto: *San'ichi shobo*, 1949.

KONG FAN-LI and QI ZHI-PING. eds. *Lu You juan*, Shanghai: *Zhong-hua shu-ju*, 1962.

**153**

LIANG RONG-RUO, ed. *Wen-xue shi-jia-zhuan*, Taizhong: Fu-ren University, 1966.

LIU WEI-CHONG, *Lu You ping-zhuan*, Taipei: *Zheng-zhong shu-ju*, 1966.

OU XIAO-MU, *Ai-guo shi-ren Lu You*, Shanghai: *Gu-dian wen-xue chu-ban-she*, 1957.

QI ZHI-PING, *Lu You*, Shanghai: *Zhong-hua shu-ju*, 1961.

————. *Lu You zhuan-lun*. Shanghai: *Zhong-hua shu-ju*, 1959.

YU BEI-SHAN, ed. *Lu You nian-pu*. Shanghai: *Zhong-hua shu-ju*, 1961.

ZHU DONG-REN. *Lu You yan-jiu*. Shanghai: *Zhong-hua shu-ju*, 1961.

————. *Lu You zhuan*. Shanghai: *Zhong-hua shu-ju*, 1960.

C. Other

LIU YI-QING *Shi-shuo xin-yu*, Shanghai: *Han-fen-lou*, 1922. *Si-bu cong-kan* edition of a fifth century book of anecdotes.

### Works in English

A. Translations and Other Works Containing Lu's Poetry

CANDLIN, CLARA M. *The Herald Wind*. London: John Murray, 1933.

————. *The Rapier of Lu, Patriot Poet of China*. London: John Murray, 1946.

LIU WU-CHI and IRVING LO, eds. *Sunflower Splendor: Three Thousand Years of Chinese Poetry*. Garden City: Doubleday Anchor, 1975.

REXROTH, KENNETH. *Love and the Turning Year*. New York: New Directions, 1970.

————. *One Hundred Poems from the Chinese*. New York: New Directions, 1971.

WALEY, ARTHUR. *Translations from the Chinese*. New York: Vintage, 1971.

WATSON, BURTON, trans. *An Introduction to Sung Poetry*. (Yoshikawa Kojiro's *Soshi Gaisetsu*.) Cambridge, Mass: Harvard University Press, 1967.

————. *The Old Man Who Does As He Pleases*. New York: Columbia University Press, 1973.

YOKE HO-PENG et al. *Lu You, The Poet Alchemist*. Canberra: Faculty of Asian Studies, Occasional Paper 13, 1972.

B. Works on Other Writers Frequently Mentioned

BIRCH, CYRIL, ED. *Anthology of Chinese Literature*. 2 vols. New York: Grove Press, 1965 and 1972.

COOPER, ARTHUR. *Li Po and Tu Fu*, Harmondsworth: Penguin, 1973.

DAVIS, A. R. *Tu Fu*, New York: Twayne, 1971.

FRODSHAM, J. D. *The Poems of Li Ho*, Oxford: Clarendon Press, 1970.

GRAHAM, A. C. *Poems of the Late T'ang*, Harmondsworth: Penguin, 1965.

HAWKES, DAVID. *Ch'u Tz'u, The Songs of the South*, Boston: Beacon Press, 1962.

————. *A Little Primer of Tu Fu*, Oxford: Clarendon Press, 1967.

HIGHTOWER, JAMES R. *The Poetry of T'ao Ch'ien*, Oxford: Clarendon Press, 1970.

LAU, D. C. *Mencius*, Harmondsworth: Penguin, 1970.

LEGGE, JAMES. *The Chinese Classics*, London: Oxford University Press, 1967. First published 1861–72.

LIU, JAMES J. Y. *The Poetry of Li Shang-yin*, Chicago: University of Chicago Press, 1969.

LO, IRVING YUCHENG. *Hsin Ch'i-chi*, New York: Twayne, 1971.

WALEY, ARTHUR. *The Analects of Confucius*, New York: Vintage, n.d.

————. *The Book of Songs*, New York: Grove Press, 1960.

————. *The Life and Times of Po Chü-i*, London: Allen and Unwin, 1949.

————. *Yuan Mei*, New York: Grove Press, n.d.

————. *Nine Songs*, London: Allen and Unwin, 1955.

WATSON, BURTON. *Chinese Lyricism*, New York: Columbia University Press, 1971.

————. *Chinese Rhymeprose*, New York: Columbia University Press, 1971.

————. *The Complete Works of Chuang Tzu*, New York: Columbia University Press, 1968.

WILHELM, RICHARD and CARY F. BAYNES. *The I Ching, or Book of Changes*, Princeton, New Jersey: Bollingen Series, XIX, 1950 and 1967.

C. On Chinese Poetry and Translation

CHEN SHOU-YI. *Chinese Literature*, New York: Ronald Press, 1961.

LIU, JAMES J. Y. *The Art of Chinese Poetry*, Chicago: University of Chicago Press, 1962.

LIU WU-CHI. *Introduction to Chinese Literature*, Bloomington: Indiana University Press, 1966.

YIP, WILLIAM WAI-LIM. *Ezra Pound's Cathay*, Princeton, New Jersey: Princeton University Press, 1969.

D. Background Works on Chinese Culture

EBERHARD, WOLFRAM. *A History of China,* revised edition, Berkeley: University of California Press, 1966.

GERNET, JACQUES. *Daily Life in China on the Eve of the Mongol Invasion, 1250–1276,* Palo Alto: Stanford University Press, 1970.

NEEDHAM, JOSEPH *et al. Science and Civilization in China,* Vol. II, Cambridge, Eng., Cambridge University Press, 1962.

SCHAFER, EDWARD H. *Ancient China,* New York: Time-Life Books, 1967.

SUZUKI, D. T. *An Introduction to Zen Buddhism,* New York: Grove Press, 1964. Originally published 1914–34.

WATSON, BURTON. *Early Chinese Literature,* New York: Columbia University Press, 1962.

E. Miscellaneous

DE ROPP, ROBERT. *The Master Game.* New York: Dell, 1968.

ELIADE, MIRCEA. *The Forge and the Crucible.* New York: Harper Torchbook, n.d. [1956 and 1962].

JAMES, WILLIAM. *The Varieties of Religious Experience.* New York: Longmans, Green and Co., 1911.

JUNG, CARL GUSTAV. *Memories, Dreams, Reflections.* New York: Vintage, 1961–63.

ROSZAK, THEODORE, ED. *Sources.* New York: Harper Colophon, 1972.

————. *Where the Wasteland Ends, Political Transcendence in Postindustrial Society.* Garden City, N. Y.: Doubleday Anchor, 1973.

WATTS, ALAN W. *Psychotherapy East and West.* New York: Ballantine, 1961.

# Index